PUBS
IN AND AROUND
YORK

PAUL CHRYSTAL

DestinWorld
publishing

For Phil and Helen, who like their York pubs

O Yorkshire, Yorkshire: Thy Ale is so strong
That it will kill us all if we stay long:
So they agreed a Journey for to make
Into the South, some Respit there to take.

(George Meriton 1684, The Praise of Yorkshire Ale)

The destroying hand of progress

(T.P. Cooper, 1897, The Old Inns and Inn Signs of York)

the death knell for many a York pub, so often the victim of myopic, and often plain stupid, corporations and city council 'decision makers', even today.

First published 2018
Destinworld Publishing Ltd
www.destinworld.com

British Library Cataloguing in Publication Data.
A catalogue record for this book is available from the British Library.

ISBN 978 1 9997175 6 8

Cover design by Ken Leeder

BY THE SAME AUTHOR

Hull Pubs

Harrogate Pubs (including Knaresborough)

Leeds's Military Heritage

York Industry Through Time

The Place Names of Yorkshire

Haworth Timelines, in press

Old Yorkshire Country Life

The Rowntree Family of York

Yorkshire Literary Landscapes

ABOUT THE AUTHOR

Paul Chrystal has Classics degrees from the Universities of Hull and Southampton; he worked as a medical publisher for nearly forty years. He is the author of eighty or so books, many of which are about York and Yorkshire. He is a regular contributor to a number of history magazines, is a reviewer for 'Classics for All', writes for a national daily newspaper, has appeared on the BBC World Service, Radio 4's PM programme and various BBC local radio stations. He lives in York.

CONTENTS

ACKNOWLEDGEMENTS

MY thanks to Ian Drake for permission to reproduce images from the Evelyn Collection, courtesy of Yorkshire Architectural and York Archaeological Society. Please go to www.yayas.org.uk and to those local breweries who took the time and trouble to send me information and images. Thanks also to Steve Lewis at York Press for permission to use images from their archive. Finally, my thanks to Katie Button at CAMRA for her help.

Every effort has been made to contact other copyright holders to gain permission to reproduce a number of the images in the book. Unfortunately, in a small number of cases no response has been forthcoming at the time of going to press. Where copyright needs to be acknowledged this will be rectified in subsequent editions where we are requested to do so.

John White (l) and Les Almond (r) in the Golden Slipper, Goodramgate, December 2017. Indefatigable research assistants.

FIRST ROUND

This is a practical beer drinker's guide to the public houses in and around the glorious city of York, a city made all the more glorious by the very pubs this book describes. Where possible, for each pub I describe its history, the origin of its name and previous names, and relevant anecdotes. The book is 'practical' because the maps show you how to get there, I give addresses, post codes, phone numbers and websites (where they exist), and I point out anything special to look for once you're there.

To make things easier for the reader, the book is organised by York's famous five bars. By bars I don't mean bars in the usual, hospitality, sense of the word: I mean the medieval gates that punctuate the city walls. So, I describe those pubs that are without – or outside – the bar and those inside, or within, that bar, and any pubs in the immediate vicinity; for example, the chapter on Monk Bar takes in the pubs on the street that is Monk Bar outside (without) and on Goodramgate, the corresponding street inside the bar and walls (within). Other centrally located pubs are then featured. We then describe pubs in the many villages around York, including, to name just a few, Haxby, Strensall and Shipton in the north; Acomb, the Pocklingtons and Nun Monkton in the west; Bishopthorpe and Fulford to the south and Dunnington and Stamford Bridge to the east.

York's brewing industry past and present is reviewed as is the important story of temperance and abstinence as it relates particularly to York. Famous stories of excessive local drinking and pub-related ghost fictions come next. The book then concludes with a sad chapter on York's lost pubs.

Space limitations mean that the book is not comprehensive, but it does feature over 160 active pubs, and some bars, making it the most extensive and detailed book on York pubs published since the late Hugh Murray's *Directory* back in 2003 when the average pub price per pint of draught bitter was £1.95.[*]

Times have indeed changed in the fifteen years since the *Directory* was published. Then, the average adult drank 218 pints per person; by 2011, that same adult downed just 152 pints, a 30 per cent drop.[**] In 2002 there were 60,100 pubs in the UK.[***] There were 50,300 pubs at the end of 2016, down from 54,194 in December 2014, according to CAMRA.

---

[*]   /www.statista.com;

[**]   telegraph.co.uk/finance/newsbysector/retailandconsumer/11283995/The-real-reasons-
        for-the-tragic-demise-of-the-British-pub-industry.html

[***]   www.beerandpub.com/statistics

Finally, just as any good pub worth its hops has a programme of guest beers, so then shall this book feature a guest pub. A pub that is not actually in York but that would grace any town or city with its unique atmosphere and ambience, exuding everything that is just right about an English pub. That guest pub, this surrogate York pub, is just up the road in Harrogate; it is, of course, the inimitable Hales Bar.

In short, I hope that the wealth of detail relating to many of the pubs included will entertain and, at the same time, give the reader a sense of the city's history, albeit an oblique and unusual but, nevertheless, compelling sense of the history of York and its surrounding villages.

A word of caution: information is correct at time of going to press, but pubs are closing or being inflicted with a change of use all the time, so please do check the latest situation if setting out to visit.

INTRODUCTION

there is nothing that has yet been contrived by man, by which so much happiness is produced, as by a good tavern or inn.

(Samuel Johnson 1709–1784)

In the days before Sat Nav, if you stopped and asked a stranger the way to somewhere, anywhere, you would most likely be directed by way of the local church (if there was one) or via the local pub or pubs. Generally speaking, pubs are still, despite it all, the second most ubiquitous feature of most high streets, be they urban or rural or suburban. That tells you just how important pubs are to any local community; like churches, they can be the focal point of a street, estate, village, town or city centre. Like churches they can, for some, satisfy a very real need for refuge, companionship, comfort and joy.

Pubs and their names, like the names of towns and villages, hills, fields, rivers and dales, often tell us much about local history in the vicinity, famous local people and local topography. This book gives a selection of some of the more interesting pubs with a tale to tell in York and in the surrounding villages. Some are still with us, others are long gone – but those that are closed are often just as vocal about the past as those whose doors remain open.

In 1875 Yorkshire could boast some 10,000 pubs. Now there are significantly fewer, with time being called for the last time all the time. The message I offered in my book on the pubs of Harrogate and Knaresborough is just as valid here:

> So, if there is a message to take away from this book it is simply put the book down, get up, go out and call in at your local for a pint or two and help preserve and extend this most British of social institutions. Once the pub, your favourite pub, has gone, it's often gone for good.

But don't take it from me – in the words of no less an authority than the ever-cautious Hilaire Belloc (1870 –1953):

> When you have lost your inns drown your empty selves for you will have lost the last of England.

He's right. Ask any villager whose local has been erased from the face of the main street.

How did our pubs come about? In the beginning, pubs, particularly pubs out in the country, brewed their own ale in brewhouses next to the pub; women often did most of the work: Madam Bradley of Northallerton and Nanny Driffield of Easingwold are veritable legends in their own brewhouses; 'Brewsters', or 'alewives' brewed ale in the home for domestic consumption and commercial sale, albeit on a small scale. These brewsters made a substantial and vital contribution to the family income. It was good ale that attracted neighbours into their houses and eventually led to the birth of the public house.

Stingo, Knockerdown and Rumtum were famous strong Yorkshire brews with well-earned reputations as far south as London's Marylebone. Stingo even had pubs named after it. Hopped ale was imported from Flanders around 1400, after which hops were home-grown in England for beer production: ale usually has a lower hop content than beer.

At the same time, hostelries were set up by the roadside catering for travellers. This had started with the Persians and Hellenistic Greeks in the 2nd century ce and perfected by the Romans locating *tabernae* on their extensive road network to proffer wine to marching legions and various other travellers. Essentially, this *cursus publicus*, public way, was made up of thousands of posting stations along the major road systems of the empire where riders and travellers took food and refreshment and horses were watered, shoed, cared for by vets, stabled, and passed over to fresh dispatch riders. Vehicles were garaged here and the taverns provided for merchants, refugees, magistrates or court officials in transit between cities.

Catering on the hoof continued apace with merchants from the Middle Ages plying between markets, as well as long-distance drovers, commercial travellers, monks commuting from monastery to monastery, pilgrims (as exemplified by *Chaucer's Canterbury Tales*) and all manner of other people moving from village to village or from town to town. Lords of the manor sometimes provided refreshing and sustaining beer-house facilities for the thirsty workers toiling in their fields.

Ale was an important part of the York diet, being as it was affordable, and unpolluted unlike water. It is estimated that the average adult then drank up to eight pints a day. Taverns, though, got off to a bad start around York when Ecgbert, Archbishop of York, around 735 ce declared ale houses to be off limits and decreed that 'no priest go to eat or drink in taverns'. Nevertheless, during King Alfred's reign (871–899) alehouses proliferated, identifiable by the ale stake – a long pole stuck outside along with a bush if wine was also on offer. In 997 ce alehouses, and their tendency to foster anti-social behaviour, entered the statute book when King Ethelred (979–1013) tried to put a price on drink-fuelled disorder with an edict that stated 'in the case of a breach of the peace in an alehouse 6 half marks shall be paid if a man is slain'. He introduced prohibition when he closed down many a tavern and restricted them to one per village. He was also the inadvertent inventor of the drinking game tradition when he introduced pegs in drinking horns – the drinker was not to go beyond the next peg with each draught. The 1215 Magna Carta had a go at establishing 'standard measures of wine and corn'. In 1267 the Assize of Ale and Bread was the first attempt, by Edward III, to establish the price of ale and minimise extortionate overpricing 'for the relief of those coming to York, and staying in the city'. It laid down conditions on brewers and ale wives, taverners and hostelers (innkeepers). From this we start to see a distinction between inns, taverns and alehouses: innkeepers provided accommodation for travellers, taverners bought wine from vintners (wine wholesalers) and resold it to their customers for consumption of their premises, ale brewers sold ale to alehouse keepers for resale in the alehouse. Licensees of ale houses were later described as tipplers and ale drapers.

Around 1319 we know from the Register of Freemen of York that the ale industry was alive and well: there were forty-seven brewers and ninety-eight taverners, hostelers and innkeepers. Alehouses, transient and low-rent, are not recorded. From 1552–1605 the mighty three-volume *Book of Recognizances Entered into by Brewers, Innholders, Tipplers and Others* identifies fifty-eight licences in Bootham, forty-one in Monk and ninety-two in Walmgate wards (none recorded for Micklegate though they obviously did exist). By 1562 the 'numbers had settled down to forty-four in Bootham, twenty-one in Micklegate, twenty-four in Monk and fifty in Walmgate. In 1596 there were eighty-three brewers, one hundred and three tipplers and sixty-four innholders. In 1663 there were 263 alehouse keepers. Between 1604 and 1966 the number of York licenses fluctuated between 194 and 155 with high points in 1683 (263) and 1896 (243), the latter to coincide with a significant rise in the city's population. In 1683 the population was around 10,000, corresponding to one drinking establishment per thirty-nine people.

Just watching one of York's world famous Mystery Plays from 1415 would show that vintners, taverners and the hostelers had their own guilds – the former performing in scenes of the Coronation of the Virgin Mary, the latter at the Marriage at the Feast of Cana. Alehouse keepers did not qualify for a guild, presumably because of the rowdiness associated with their establishments and their lowly position in the social order.

In 1393 Richard II introduced more regulation when he saw the tax potential to be had in ale and decreed that 'whosoever shall brew in the town with the intention of selling it must hang out a sign'. In so doing he not only gave birth to the fine tradition of pub signage, he also made life easy for his revenue men and for law enforcers to spot potential tax and trouble. Hitherto, most early ale houses were located in private houses, so there was no need for regulation or the signage that went with it.

Richard II's action also explains why many pub names have associations with the Wars of the Roses (1455–1487) – Rose & Crown, White Hart, Blue Boar, and so on; the decree came relatively soon before the start of the war, which will have provided a source of fresh, new names. Thanks to their continued unsavoury reputation, alehouses later got sucked into 1496 legislation relating to 'vagabonds, idle and suspected persons' when justices of the peace gained powers to 'rejecte and put away common ale selling in townes and places where they shall think convenyent'. In 1552 keepers of alehouses and tippling houses were required to be licensed; tippling houses were places where beer could be sold but not brewed.

Things got serious in York in 1562 when the Corporation instructed parish constables to compile lists of all the ale and tippling houses in their parishes from which the Lord Mayor would imperiously decide which could continue in their trade. Bowling alleys, too, were listed as were all inhabitants, particularly the indigent, impotent and aged. And so the census was born, although it did look more like an early attempt at pious social cleansing. Those drinking establishments lucky enough to win approval – and survival – were required not to allow the playing of dice, cards, bowls or shovegroat; church congregations were reminded that it was *verboten* to enter a tavern or alehouse or tippling house after 9 p.m. or on Sundays or festivals; penalty: a minimum of three days in prison.

By the mid-16th century there were 19,759 taverns or inns in England and Wales, or 1:187 people compared with 1:650 today.

In York in the Middle Ages the saying goes that there was a monastery for every day of the week (7), a church for every week of the year (52) and a pub for every day of the year (365). Believe it or not, this is only a slight exaggeration as there were seven major monastic houses, forty-five or so churches, and about 200 inns and alehouses. We meet some of the men who ran the very early alehouses in the 1277 Roll of Freedmen; publicans listed there include William de Castleford, Adam de Pontefract, Rogerus de Wambewell, William de Whityngton and Johannes de Appelby – taverners all. William the Inkeeper, however, had appeared in the 1250s list of Vicars Choral. The 1301 Civic Ordinances list a number of law-breaking hostelers. A charter from between 1180 and 1240 gives us Ketell Bracarius, brewer.

The George in Coney Street is the first York pub to be recorded – in 1455 as Hospicium Georgii. In 1459 the nearby Bull was mentioned in a Corporation Ordinance. Other 15th century pubs recorded include the Crowned Lion (1483), the Dragon (1484), the Boar (1485) and the Swan (1487). Names were simple then.

A word of caution. The dates of pubs can be misleading. It is important to distinguish between the date of the building, which may have had a myriad of uses, and the date of licensing. So, for example, the Old Black Swan in Peasholme Green, and the Red Lion, Merchantgate, both date to the 15th–16th century and as such are probably the oldest buildings in York operating as pubs, but have only become pubs quite recently; on the other hand, the Golden Fleece, Pavement, has been licensed continuously since 1668, although it was rebuilt in the 19th century.

Very early sketches of the Black Swan, back and front views.
The front view dates from 1809. (Evelyn Collection, courtesy of
Yorkshire Architectural and York Archaeological Society)

The oldest continuously licensed premises in York are:

1. Olde Starre, Stonegate – 1644
2. Golden Fleece, Pavement – 1668
3. Old White Swan, Goodramgate – 1703
4. Robin Hood (formerly Little John), Castlegate – 1733
5. Punch Bowl, Stonegate – 1761
6. Windmill, Blossom Street – 1770

The Golden Fleece and The Punch Bowl

In the 16th century, as the number of pubs increased, so did the drink fuelled disorder – and the legislation that went with it. The nine York inn-holders (hostellers) in 1550 had swelled to sixty-four inn-holders and 103 alehouse keepers by 1596. The Alehouses Act of 1551 was a central government attempt to deal with the 'abuses and disorders as are had and used in common ale houses'. Justices of the Peace could apply sanctions to rowdy establishments enabled as they were 'to remove, discharge and put away common selling of ale and beer'.

The apparent problem with taverns was that that there was deemed to be too many of them and that the wine served was usually of dubious quality. So, in 1553 the number of taverns was restricted by law: London was allowed forty, York a mere eight and Hull and other comparable sized cities a miserable four. However, legislation so universally, yet gleefully, ignored and unenforced would be hard to find: in 1623 there were still 13,000 licensed premises in England.

In 1562 the legislation mentioned above gave the Corporation of York powers to grant licences to 139 innholders and brewers allowing them to continue brewing ale. In 1572 Elizabeth's Council of the North, established in York, demanded yet more robust regulation; in 1604 legislation – An Act to Restrain the Inordinate Haunting and Tippling of Inns, Alehouses, and Other Drinking Places – was passed to redefine the very role of drinking establishments: they were definitely *not* for 'Entertainment and Harbouring lewd and idle People to spend and consume their Time in lewd and drunken Manner'. What they were for was the 'Receipt, Relief and Lodging of Wayfaring people from place to place'. Having fun, social cohesion and community then, were officially subsidiary to the provision of board and lodge. Ironically, and awkwardly, things then became very confusing when tipplers were required by law to 'serve all the Queen's people, without refusal for their ready money'; trouble makers or not, they had to be served.

In this blizzard of well-meaning but ineffective legislation, evasion was rife, especially illegal brewing and keeping an alehouse without a licence; the production of illicit ale was far too profitable for it not to be; the corollary to this was the effect of strong beer on the temper and temperament, effects that were all too predictable. And so the bar room brawling continued.

But it was by no means wall-to-wall violence. In her 1698 *Through England on a Side Saddle in the Time of William and Mary* the enterprising and fearless Celia Fiennes called in at York in 1697. The intrepid lady traveller journeyed the length and breadth of the country, often with only one or two maids in attendance. This is how she described the River 'Ouise' and the mean streets of York

> it bears Great Barges, it Looks muddy, its full of good ffish. We Eate very good Cod fish and Salmon and that at a pretty Cheape rate, tho' we were not in the best jnn for the Angel is the best in Cunny Streete. The houses are very Low and as jndifferent as in any Country town and the Narrowness of ye Streetes makes it appear very mean.

A few years later Daniel Defoe, in his *A Tour Through the Whole Island of Great Britain*, concurs:

> There is abundance of good company here, and abundance of good families live here, for the sake of the good company and cheap living; a man converses here with all the world as effectually as at London.

Nevertheless, in the ongoing battle against illicit production and rowdiness some progress appears to have been made by 1743; new laws restricted the issuing of licences to keepers of public houses (not chandlers and grocers and the like); only one licence could be held, licences could only be issued at Brewster Sessions and transfers at Transfer Sessions, licensees had to be of a higher social standing and were required to produce sureties of good behaviour.

Coffee Houses

A degree of civilisation and sobriety came with the emergence of the coffee house. Coffee houses of all complexions – salubrious and salacious alike – were all the rage in the 17th and 18th centuries. Coffee houses were not just about coffee drinking. The more civilised establishments were not only convivial, sober and convenient places to meet for artists, politicians, dandies about town and writers; serious business and banking transactions took place in them; Freemasons had their Lodge meetings there. It was said that in a coffee house a man could 'pick up more useful knowledge than by applying himself to his books for a whole month'. Crucially, beer and spirits were to be had there too, to help lubricate the free exchange of news and information.

However, burgeoning coffee shops being essentially what they were, the sales of non-alcoholic beverages had serious economic implications for the Exchequer and for farmers. Farmers saw tea, coffee and brandy as unwelcome competition for their wheat, barley and malt – constituents of beer – and wanted them banned. When a man was in a coffee house, he was not downing ale in an alehouse. In the 3,000 or so coffee houses operating in the land in 1675, coffee was being ordered in preference to the traditional glass of ale or gin – alcoholic beverages from which the Government received substantial tax revenues. Pascal Rosee, London coffee shop pioneer, alone sold over 600 dishes of coffee a day at the very dawn of the coffee revolution.

There was a plethora of coffee houses in York from 1669 when there are at least thirty recorded: amongst these were Parker's in Minster Yard – next to a bowling alley as shown on Horsley's 1896 map; the Garrick in Low Petergate; Wombwell and Wink's; Harrison's in Petergate and later Nessgate; Iveson's, also in Petergate, Duke's near the Ouse Bridge; and Brigg's on the corner of Stonegate and Coffee Yard – as well as William Tuke's roasting house. As one of thirty-one York tea dealers in 1823 and importers of tea, coffee and chocolate, the Tuke family were the exclusive holders in the north of England of a licence that permitted the processing of coffee beans and the sale of roasted coffee, tea and chocolate. Chicory was grown around York for a time in the 19th century and purchased by merchants who sold it on as an additive to coffee. One such merchant was Henry Wilberforce (d. 1876) of Walmgate, succeeded by his son William Wilkinson Wilberforce, Mayor in 1880.

Coffee Yard off Stonegate with the printer's devil frowning down, indicative of the publishing industry in the area – so often associated with coffee houses.

Coaching, Trains and the Motor Car

Things started to change nationally in the 17th century when in 1657 turnpikes led to a huge increase in the number of horses and coaches full of passengers criss-crossing the country. In 1663 York, something of a hub, could offer 263 licensed public houses; by 1700 there was one drinking place for every thirty-nine people, growth demanded by the accommodation, feeding and watering of the newly mobile travelling public. Turnpikes demanded coaching inns for board and lodge for the drivers and passengers, and stabling for the horses, which required regular changing. The railways 200 years later brought the next seismic change with the establishment of railway inns at stations; a third development was the now ubiquitous motor car and the transportation of goods by road, all of which necessitated catering for day trippers, business people, long-distance lorry drivers and other travellers – often in the very pubs that once served coach and railway travellers.

Brewhouses

The first common brewers were the Nesfield family of Scarborough established in 1691; the end of the 18th century saw the emergence of the common brewery;

this was boosted by Wellington's Beerhouse Act of 1830 with names from the 19th century like Hull Brewery, John Smith's, Sam Smith's, Tetley's, Timothy Taylor's and Theakston's, most still very much alive in the 20th century and, in some cases, into this century. Beer brewing had moved out of the home and was an industry in its own right, supplying a growing number of public houses and hotels.

The aim of the Beerhouse Act was to encourage people to drink beer rather than spirits, gin mainly. Any householder that paid the poor rate could sell beer, ale or porter by buying an excise licence; they did not a need a justices' licence but spirit-selling retailers did. Sellers of ale had to promise to give correct measures, maintain good order, to allow no drunkenness or gambling, and not to dilute the beer! The Beerhouse Act abolished the beer tax, and extended the opening hours of licensed public houses, taverns and alehouses to from fifteen to eighteen hours a day.

The Act also gave rise to the beerhouse and beershops that were permitted to sell only beer. Opening hours could be from 4 a.m. to 10 p.m. – good for a breakfast pint. For 2 guineas payable to the local excise officer, anyone could now brew and sell beer. The excise licence would stipulate whether the beer could be consumed on the premises (beerhouse) or as off-sales only (beershop). Supervision by local justices was severely curtailed leading to complaints by magistrates and local gentry keen to control the working classes in their area.

Not everyone warmed to the Act, driving the making of beer underground, doing nothing for the fight against intoxication: many beerhouses emerged from the back streets of large cities and became working class drinking dens. The Leeds Mercury of 23 October 1830 reported, 'We receive from many quarters grievous complaints of the demoralising effects of this Act, which has, by making beer cheap, led to an increase of intoxication'.

The Beerhouse Act of 1830 saw licensed premises double in ten years with 24,000 new licences issued within three months of the legislation. It also galvanised the rise and rise of the common brewery, brewing beer and selling it to other outlets rather than brewing for oneself.

In 1823 Hull had 274 inns serving a population of 44,924 making one pub per 164 people; York was even better provisioned with 194 inns for 22,529 inhabitants: one for every 116 residents. Take children out of the equation and the figures are even more astonishing. Tadcaster takes the biscuit in 1837 with twenty-four inns and taverns and eleven beerhouses: thirty-five places to drink for a population of 2,400, providing one pub for every seventy people – more than twice the national average at the time. At its peak, Sheffield in 1863 had 560 inns and hotels with 682 beerhouses and over 600 off licences. Beerhouses naturally proliferated around the steel mills and heavy engineering factories: a common sight was boys wielding broomsticks with cans suspended full of beer for the thirsty workers.

Beerhouses provided not just beer, but food, games and some even lodging. They were also known by the name 'small beer' or 'Tom and Jerry' shops. In villages and towns many shopkeepers opened their own beershop and sold beer alongside their usual wares. Beer would be brewed on the premises or purchased from brewers.

Many beerhouses inevitably became the haunt of criminals and prostitutes, with some eliding into thinly disguised brothels. The official reaction was to raise the excise fee to 3 guineas and to introduce property qualifications. But only the Wine and Beer House Act of 1869 brought the licensing of the beerhouses back under the control of the local justices. Many then closed, or were purchased by breweries and changed to fully licensed public houses.

Pubs were never always just pubs. Many doubled up as coroners' and magistrates' courts, as markets, morgues and as smugglers' dens; smugglers always drank in the Ship in Saltburn; others were also blacksmith's, cobblers or carpenters – often the landlord's day job. The Denmark Arms in Scarborough was also a grocer's until its closure. Appropriately enough, The White Boar in Huddersfield was also a butcher's; fiddling the customer has always happened: in 1734 the landlord here, John Walker, was fined for giving short measures. The Beaumont Arms at Kirkheaton near Huddersfield doubled as an undertakers. The Three Nuns at Mirfield was where the local nuns brewed their own ale. The Cricket Inn in Sheffield's Hyde Park had its own cricket pitch from 1826, as has The Strafford Arms at Stainborough nearby. The Victoria Park Hotel in Sheffield had a bowling green and 'an American bowling alley' in the mid 1800s. The Crooked Billet at Ryhill near Hedon housed a slaughterhouse. Best of all, though, was The Humber Tavern in Paull east of Hull; here, in 1836 Trinity House decided that 'lights be exhibited in the windows of a public house at Paull as a temporary expedient until the erection of permanent lights'.

Pub Signs

Pub signs and the names and the images depicted on them make an intriguing subject all of their own. The Romans started it all with a welcoming sign showing a bunch of vine leaves representing the wine god Bacchus to denote a *taberna* – *the* place for a legionary, government official, itinerant or a merchant to slake his thirst. As with any other commercial enterprise, pubs use signs or symbols to signify the nature of the business going on within. The barber's pole and the pawnbroker's balls still survive to this day: the reason for all this symbolism was that until the end of the 19th century most people could not read, so word signage would have been quite useless: a symbolic, graphic sign, however, clearly spoke volumes. For pubs, a garland on a pole, the ale-stake, denoted a place where drink could be had. Red lattices on glassless windows also gave the game away for what was on offer within.

  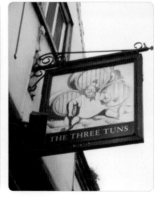

From 1393 it was a legal requirement for innkeepers to display a sign: pub owners accordingly invented names and signs to differentiate their pub from the one up the road: your sign set you apart from other inns and taverns in the locality; it might also advertise what might be found inside (for example, cold meats or board games as well as ale), or indeed the political leanings of the landlord and his clientele. Coats of arms reflect the custom adopted by noblemen in which they displayed their banners outside the inn to show that they might be found within. York's imposing gallows sign at Ye Olde Starre Inne spanning Stonegate is a very rare surviving example of these literally unmissable pub indicators.

However, York's oldest is the (long gone) George, or *Hospicium Georgii* recorded in a 1455 will; after that was 'the sign of the Bull in Conyng Street' from a Corporation Ordinance and, separately, in the Ouse Bridge Master's Accounts both in 1459. The Bull's sign showed the badge of the Clarence family; other regal or heraldic badges on pub signs include the Crowned Lion (1483), the royal crest; the Dragon (1484), the badge of Edward IV indicating a Tudor supporter; the Boar (1485) Richard III; the Swan (1487) Henry IV. Then there was the Mitford in 1489. Religion then became a fashionable motif with the Three Kings in 1554 and the Star in 1580.

The name Royal Oak indicated a supporter of Charles II (he hid in an oak at Boscobel after the battle of Worcester in 1651 before restoring the monarchy in 1660); Punch Bowl denoted a Whig establishment and their patrons' predilection for punch. Though rebuilt in 1931, the Punch Bowl in Stonegate (one of at least three in York) goes back to 1675 as a coffee house. It was a meeting place for the Whig political party (precursors of the Liberals) who drank punch, hence the name. The Tories still preferred port and red wines. It has been licensed continuously since 1761, so it is the fifth oldest pub in York. It was the HQ of the York Race Committee and the resort of York Minster bell-ringers in the 18th century.

Marquis of Granby reflected the philanthropy of said Marquis to his veterans. Chequers denoted board games available while The Board proclaimed that cold meats were on offer inside – the board being what the meats were served on, hence 'board and lodge'.

As stated above, pub names are a fascinating study all of their own and York's names are no exception. Animals abound in the naming of our pubs: North of York, Haxby and the contiguous village of Wigginton are a veritable safari park with their Tiger, Red Lion and Black Horse. Foxes abound, with or without the hounds; one Fox is in Holgate in York, another was in Low Petergate dating from the 15th century but demolished in 1958; its other names were The Lord Byron and The Beech Tree. There's also a Fox lurking in Stockton-on-the Forest.

The first list of pubs comes in 1733 with Thomas Gent's 'list of carriers who inn at York' in his *Ancient and Modern History of Ripon*. Of the twenty inns listed, only three survive. Other lists followed in 1783 with three Chequers – like the Board, a catch-all name, and a list featuring three Trellises (one in Coffee Yard and one in Goodramgate). Indeed, originality was never a concern as the Blue Bell and others attest: at the time there was a whole bunch of Blue Bells in York (nine); a troop of Bay Horses (nine) and a service of Punch Bowls (seven), three of which live on.

We can estimate that 1500 or so pub names for York and the surrounding villages have existed over the years; this, of course, includes the numerous name changes made by many a pub. The Coney Street Bull is our earliest example of serial name changing when the bull turned into a Rose.

More recently, the New Inn in Stamford Bridge was renamed The Swordsman in 1974 to celebrate the town's proud Viking heritage.

Other belligerent Yorkshire pubs include The Standard Inn after the 1138 battle of that name near Northallerton; and The Crooked Billet (a twisted branch used as a poor man's walking stick or as a weapon) after the exceedingly bloody War of the Roses battle at Towton in 1461. It is the meeting place of Towton Battlefield Society, whose aim is to preserve the skills and craft of the traditional longbow. York had its Trafalgar Bay and Halifax its Trafalgar; there is a Crimea Tavern at Castleford and a Crimea Inn near Huddersfield; The Balaclava Inn was in Norton and The Inkerman Tavern in Hull. An Alma Inn at Sowerby Bridge is named after the victory at Alma in the Crimea. Rotherham's Tabard denotes the sleeveless tunics worn by heralds while The Cat and Bagpipes, a corruption of cateran, at East Harlsey reminds us of the marauding, freebooting Scots. Darsfield near Barnsley has The Longbow. Todmorden celebrates two ships involved in a naval battle outside Boston Harbour during the American War of Independence: The Chesaspeake and Shannon, which opened in 1813. The outcome was that The Shannon captured The Chesaspeake and towed her to Halifax, Nova Scotia where she was commissioned into the Royal Navy. There is a Dunkirk Inn at Denby Dale. The Light Horseman in York from 1830 echoes to the building of the cavalry barracks nearby in Fulford Road.

In York there have been seven Lord, or Admiral, Nelsons; a number of Wellingtons around the Napoleonic Wars with timely promotions to Lord, Marquis and Duke of Wellington. The Alma Terrace Wellington ejected the general Sir Colin Campbell. Tanner Row's Sun Inn was named after the admiral Sir Sidney Smith in 1818 before going back to the Sun. Smith (1764–1840) served in the American and French revolutionary wars. Napoleon said of him: 'That man made me miss my destiny.' New monarchs were popular with six Queen Victorias in the city.

Pub names could be personal. When Christopher Barthorpe, licensee of the Hare and Hounds (later the Bay Malton, Bay Horse, Cornerstones and Keystones) moved to the Old George in Pavement he took the name with him. Barthorpe was City Huntsman at the time. Thomas Moon stamped his mark on his new Walmgate pub, which was formerly the Barleycorn and the Hope and Anchor when he rebadged it in 1838 the Full Moon. Christopher Bean, ex-polar harpooner, changed the name of his pub to the Whale Fishery in 1843 from the Oddfellows Arms in Hungate. A pub named all things barrel-related – the Barrel Churn (1873), The Cooper (1788), The Barrel (1818) converted to the Mail Coach in 1834 when a former mail coach driver took charge.

Nicknames sometimes prevailed. The Corner Pin in Tanner Row assumed precedence over the Unicorn (also the Oddfellows Arms in 1838–1841). An 1852 Ordnance Survey map shows the Cannon but it was always better known as the Gun: the picture on the sign would, to all intents and purposes, show just a gun.

The Old George in Pavement around 1949.

Rubbish beer may have been responsible for the naming of the Putrid Arms in Skeldergate in an 1818 street directory.

The St Nicholas (later the Burns' Hotel in 1902) in Lawrence Street may have been renamed the Tam O'Shanter after the Chester Cup winner in 1876, although it was probably named after the Robert Burns poem.

Antiquity, or the suggestion of antiquity, has been a factor in at least twenty-one name changes down the years, as a prefix. The Duke's Head in Aldwark is a case in point, in a case of some Byzantine complexity. It opened in 1823 as the Duke of York but was sometimes called the Duke's Head after a literal rendition of what you saw on the sign. When Robert Merrington moved next door he called his new pub the Old Duke's Head to differentiate it from the new pub that opened in his old premises and was named the Duke's Head. To make things even clearer, Merrington sometimes called his Old Duke's Head the Original Duke's Head. Life became much simpler on Aldwark when the Old Duke's Head closed in 1806 and the Duke's Head continued unopposed as the Duke's Head.

Working Men's and Other Clubs

Within the city walls there were three working men's clubs in the 1960s – thirty around the city as a whole. They were St Clement's in Queen Victoria Street,

Vickers Instruments in Bishophill and York British Legion at 61 Micklegate. Down the road a maximum of forty people at any one time were allowed in The 55 Club for drinking and gambling in a Georgian ambience. The Old World Club opened in Stonegate in the wake of the failed Raceways club with gaming, dining and dancing in the basement. Tiffanys toyed with their menu and moved upmarket from the Wimpy-type menus. The Society Club in Bootham was deemed the best place to eat with 'other facilities' for members in other rooms. What would neighbours Rowntrees have thought?

A club in the 1920s opposite the Mason's Arms in Fishergate on the left. (Evelyn Collection, courtesy of Yorkshire Architectural and York Archaeological Society)

The Student View

Socially speaking, a quick pint after work, particularly on Fridays, has always been a popular and, for many, an essential event. An article in the 1960s student magazine, *Eboracum*, described a typical night out:

> The White Horse and The Market Tavern, The Lendal Bridge, The Coach & Horses, and others, are at weekends packed to capacity with young people from York and the villages outside, flash girls, farm workers, hard men and rockers. The rock pubs are all things to all men. A rumble is the easiest. An air of frustrated violence fills the already crowded bars and a spilled drink, a casual glance at an unknown girl, a 'joke' is enough excuse for a fight. Walking down Coppergate between eleven and twelve on a Saturday night can be frightening and, occasionally, dangerous.

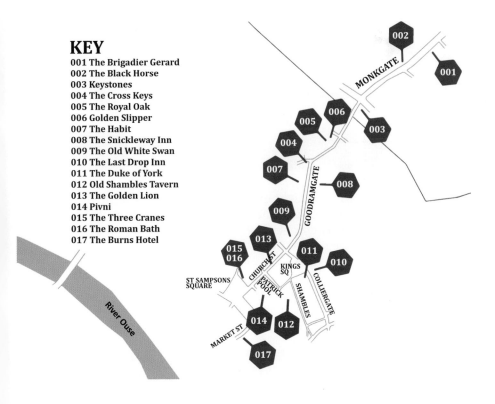

KEY

001 The Brigadier Gerard
002 The Black Horse
003 Keystones
004 The Cross Keys
005 The Royal Oak
006 Golden Slipper
007 The Habit
008 The Snickleway Inn
009 The Old White Swan
010 The Last Drop Inn
011 The Duke of York
012 Old Shambles Tavern
013 The Golden Lion
014 Pivni
015 The Three Cranes
016 The Roman Bath
017 The Burns Hotel

MONK BAR

We now begin our bar-based tour of the pubs and a few bars in and around York.

Built around 1330 Monk Bar was originally called Monkgate Bar; at sixty-three feet it is the tallest of York's Bars. Designed as a self-contained fortress, assailants had to cross each floor to reach the next flight of stairs, thus exposing themselves to defensive fire. The Bar features loopholes (for bows and arrows); gun ports and murder holes from which heavy objects and boiling water might be dropped. The coat of arms is Plantagenet. The Bar was used as a prison in the 16th century for recusant Catholics, and others: in 1588 Robert Walls was imprisoned for 'drawing blood in a fray'. The barbican was removed in the early 1800s. To rent the rooms at the top, one Thomas Pak (Master Mason at the Minster) paid 4s per annum. Little Ease was a tiny prison cell in Monk Bar little over five feet in diameter. In 1594 Alice Bowman, a local recusant, was held here. From 1845 to 1913 a police inspector lived there, and in other rooms. It is now part of the Richard III Museum in the Bar.

Goodramgate is named after Guthrum, a Danish chief active around 878 ce. The Grade I listed Lady Row cottages (numbers 60–72) dates from 1316. They are the oldest surviving jettied cottages in Britain. Originally nine or ten houses for the priests at neighbouring Holy Trinity church, the one at the southern end was demolished in 1766 to make way for a gateway to the 13th to 15th century Holy Trinity church. They each comprised one room ten by fifteen feet on each floor. Rents collected went to pay for chantries to the Blessed Virgin Mary in nearby churches. Two pubs occupied the cottages at various times: The Hawk's Crest from 1796–1819 and The Noah's Ark around 1878.

Lady Row cottages.

THE BRIGADIER GERARD

Monkgate
84 Monkgate, York YO31 7PF
01904 642612

A private residence and the Gas Works Social Club were previous uses for this school building, which was extended and converted into 'The Brigadier Gerard' in 1984. The name comes from the famous racehorse (1968–1989), a pre-eminent British thoroughbred and sire that won the 2,000 guineas in 1971 and seventeen of its eighteen races – the only defeat was at York in 1972. He is considered the best racehorse trained in Britain in the 20th century. The horse, in turn, was named after Brigadier Etienne Gerard, the hero in Arthur Conan Doyle's *Exploits of Brigadier Gerard,* a series of short stories originally published in *The Strand* magazine between 1894 and 1903.

The Brigadier Gerard in the early 21st and early 20th centuries.

THE BLACK HORSE

Monkgate
29 Monkgate, York YO31 7PB
01904 620284

Called the Tap and Spile from 1988, this fine late Victorian pub from 1822 was rebuilt in 1897 and has in 2017 reverted to the name it had for the ninety-one years before that: The Black Horse. The stonework on the outside is superb, as are the tiles on the inside, particularly around the mirrors behind the bar. Book-filled bookcases and an elegant fire place add to the character of this Flemish style building.

KEYSTONES (formerly The Bay Horse)

Monkgate
4 Monkgate, York, YO31 7PE
01904 656202
www.screampubs.co.uk/thekeystonesYork

A pub in the shadow of the bar under the city walls. The Ice House – a brick-lined vaulted early 19th century edifice is nearby; it was used for the storage of winter ice which, in turn, would be used for the cooling and preservation of food and drink in the summer. The Ice House is accessible from the pub garden.

Keystones with Monk Bar lit up for Christmas 2017.

THE CROSS KEYS

Goodramgate
34 Goodramgate, York YO1 7LF
01904 655082

This is an early Edwardian pub from 1904 in orange brick. When a section of Goodramgate was knocked down to create Deangate, an earlier Cross Keys, with records going back to 1783, went with it.

Cross keys are a common symbol in York, particularly in the vicinity of the Minster: they are St Peter's keys to heaven, the St Peter to whom York Minster is dedicated – the Cathedral and Metropolitical Church of St Peter in York. St Peter's keys are prominent in York Minster's logo. The area around the Minster nearby was the Liberty of St Peter: in medieval times, this was administered by the Dean and Chapter of the Minster and not by the city's Lord Mayor. The walls enclosing the Liberty were twelve feet high, broken only by four guarded gates; inside were the Archbishop's Palace, the Dean's house and houses for the Canons, the Treasurer and the Precentor (together they form The Chapter), and St William's College. The pub boasts some fine etched frosted glass windows.

The original Cross Keys is on the right before it was demolished to make way for Deangate around 1910. In those days this was the A64 Leeds to Scarborough road via the Minster and railway station. The Steigmann brothers were butchers, immigrants from Germany who came to York in 1870.

THE ROYAL OAK

Goodramgate
18 Goodramgate, York YO1 7LG
01904 628869
www.royaloakYork.co.uk/history/

The Royal Oak York is a Grade II listed building. The excellent website informs us that the timbered building is 15th century when it was probably a local merchant's house. It was first recorded as a pub in 1772 when John Dickinson was the first landlord, although it is thought to have been an inn for many years before this. In 1783 Charles Popplewell was in charge of what was then The Blue Pig; eleven years later it was renamed The Blue Boar or Boar under a John Furness. John Kilby, a future Mayor of York, took over in 1797 and owned it for over twenty years until he was declared bankrupt. The summer of 1819 saw the rights to the pub auctioned in the Robin Hood in Castlegate with Thomas Belt's winning bid of £460. By 1825 it was known as the Royal Oak and taken over in 1828 by Robert Bowman until 1849 when The Oak passed to Robert Bateman; his wife Ellen ran the pub from 1858 – Robert's death – until 1871, when her son-in-law, William Shutt of Harrogate, became licensee. William had married Jane Bateman and the couple ran the pub together until 1881 when William passed away. Widow Jane then took over the running of the pub. In 1886, Robert Bateman Jr – son of Robert and Ellen – abandoned his trade as a butcher to run The Royal Oak with his wife, Elizabeth.

In 1894 the John J. Hunt Brewery – on nearby Aldwark – bought the pub and installed Walter Dodgson as landlord. When Leonard Coates became landlord in 1898 his large wooden sign above the doorway simply bore his name. In 1934 John J. Hunt Brewery closed the pub briefly to fit it out with the mock Tudor interior we enjoy to this day. A library adds to the atmosphere.

GOLDEN SLIPPER

Goodramgate

20 Goodramgate, York YO1 7LG
www.davidnewtoninteractive.co.uk
01904 651235

Records for a Shoe or Shou here reach back to 1795. It was the Slipper in 1818 and the Golden Slipper in 1823.

'To create the unique ambience of an English country pub, but in the very heart of the beautiful City of York.' That's the aim of the current owners of this wonderful pub. The northeastern part of the pub was built in the 15th and 16th centuries while the 19th century saw the rest completed and the Victorian brick facade added. The pub website adds some fascinating detail:

In 1821 a William Brown was hanged on Bailie Hill for robbing John Armstrong when he was returning from having a few on the sign of 'The Slipper in Goodramgate'. Armstrong had been soundly beaten and dumped in the river until he was 'still and stagnated with cold' (*The Gazette* 17–24 March 1821).

In April 1826 the *York Herald* reported a 'Strike amongst the bricklayers – A meeting was held at Mrs March's, at the sign of The Slipper in Goodramgate, on Wednesday last'. Employers got together to reduce the wages of the journey men by two shillings per week – a reduction that the men refused to accept and a 'strike' was the outcome.

In 1984 during alteration works workmen found a mediaeval leather slipper, one of a pair of two that was built into 14th century buildings to ward off evil spirits; it is now displayed in the front snug lounge. The other shoe would have belonged to a child, but is yet to be found. Some argue

Note the giant gilded slipper

The Golden Slipper in 1989.

that the pub is named after a greyhound.

Still in the front lounge, you can see where a 'Coffin Drop' was located – where the ceiling is lower; it would allow corpses to exit the building via the side passage, as it was thought to be very unlucky for a body to leave from the front door of a building.

THE HABIT

Goodramgate

40 Goodramgate, York, YO1 7LF
01904 611072

The Habit inhabits a building that was made up of former stonemaker apprentices' and priests' living and working quarters; it was formerly owned by the Minster, hence the name. The quintessentially medieval atmosphere comes from the largely unspoilt rooms and the unique views of the Minster it offers from the roof terrace. The pub–café actively supports local artists – both painters and musicians.

THE SNICKLEWAY INN

Goodramgate

A 15th century pub named after the famous snickelways – alleys and backstreets – that thread through and characterise the city. The pub was once a brothel as well as seeing service as the Royalist powder magazine during the English Civil War. The stunning façade we see today was plastered over in the early 19th century.

Snickelways refer to the network of narrow pedestrian-only alleyways that spider their way through the city. The word is a neologism coined by Mark Jones in his 1983 *A Walk Around the Snickelways of York*; it is a compound of *snicket*, a walled passageway; *ginnel*, a narrow passageway between buildings, and *alleyway*, a narrow street or lane. In the words of Mark Jones, it is 'a narrow place to walk along, leading from somewhere to somewhere else, usually in a town or a city, especially in the city of York'. Indeed, they, as if by magic, connect two parts of the city seemingly completely separate and very distant from each other. In York, examples include Mad Alice Lane, Hornpot Lane, Mucky Peg Lane, Hole in the Wall, Pope's Head Alley, and Coffee Yard (Langton Lane).

The Snickleway Inn [sic], parts of which are believed to date back to the 1400s, was originally, from 1896, called The Angler's Arms, nothing to do with fishermen, because it was close to the Minster stonemasons' yard – an angler being a geometrist (someone who studies geometry) working on the stones. This follows a long tradition of the pub being named after artisans: previous names also include The Painters' Arms (18th century), The Square & Compass, The Mason's Arms and The Board (1852–1891) or Cooper's Vaults after the then owner. The current name was adopted in 1994. Note the deliberate misspelling to avoid infringing Mark Jones' copyright.

In the early 20th century one of the landladies was a Lilly Marley who had a servant with the wonderfully Dickensian name of Flora Bogitt.

Inside the inn with that magnificent tapestry.

THE OLD WHITE SWAN

Goodramgate
80 Goodramgate, York YO1 7LF
01904 540911

The Old White Swan is made up of a motley collection of buildings, part timber framed, but mainly brick, dating from the 16th century; they include a Georgian dining room to the left and a Tudor bar straight ahead as you go in. The two storied centre ranges from the 16th century, set back from street, with side wings mid-18th century. The frontage to Goodramgate was rebuilt in 1771. At one time the pub opened out onto both Petergate and Goodramgate.

The Old White Swan was recorded as an inn in 1703 but it has had multiple uses: various parts of it at various times were a pigsty, barber's shop, poultry market and barn. The Gallery and Minstrel Bar exhibit fine examples of timber framing and a former hayloft. A Roman column is preserved under a glass panel, but is not *in situ*.

The pub lay unusually in two parishes – Holy Trinity King's Court, and Holy Trinity, Goodramgate, so it paid two sets of rates. Unsurprisingly, this caused much dispute, and in the early 17th century a white line was painted through the courtyard and in through the kitchen door to show the boundary.

In 1723 during the Jacobite troubles Papists were often sought out here; one record shows how two parish constables got through £1 while on the lookout in the pub for Papists. The Old White Swan was a major coaching and posting inn in the late 18th and early 19th centuries. Before the railways, it was a popular haunt for farmers and poultry dealers, who used to collect poultry from country districts and congregate at the Old White Swan to sell them to their city clients.

When in 1742 William Barwick took over the pub – he had been licensee at the Sandhill in Colliergate – he renamed his new pub the White Swan & Sandhill, a name that stuck until 1786. This is when two side wings were added, one of which saw use as a barber shop.

In 1781, the world's tallest man, twenty-one-year-old Patrick Cotter O'Brian, was exhibited at the pub by landlord William Featherstonehaugh for an extended run. O'Brian stood eight feet and one inch tall and the then landlord charged onlookers a shilling for a gawp in the building at the back of the pub, now the kitchens. Patrick Cotter O'Brien was the first of only thirteen people in medical history to be recorded as having a height of eight feet or more. Today, he would have been diagnosed as having gigantism. *The Salem Massachusetts Gazette*, dated 15 May 1792, describes O'Brien as 'An athletic make, a great example of proportion, and justly allowed to be the greatest wonder of the age'.

O'Brien toured the world on the strength of his height, his gigantism, and died a very rich man in 1806, aged forty-six. Bequeathing £2000 to his mother, he requested that his body be buried in twelve square feet of solid rock, to avoid body snatchers exhuming it and selling it on for medical research.

Notwithstanding, in 1972, his remains were dug up and the research began. One of his arms has been preserved in the Medical Museum of the Royal College of Surgeons in London, and his huge, custom-made boots are on display at the Kinsale Museum, County Cork. In 1825 a tripe-eating contest took place here, the aim being to swallow 10 pounds in one go; however, only seven pounds was managed.

Coaching took off from the White Swan with journeys to Durham, Newcastle and Glasgow. Locally, Helperby and Easingwold were served from here. Mounting steps are still visible. In 1862 the stained-glass artist, John Ward Knowles, painted the sign that has changed little from the fine sign we see today.

The jukebox had a difficult birth in York, perhaps not that surprising if you consider the origin of the word: *jukebox* came into use in the United States in 1940, derived from the familiar usage juke joint, itself derived from the Gullah word 'juke' or 'joog' meaning disorderly, rowdy, or wicked. Gullah are descendants of enslaved Africans who live in South Carolina and Georgia. Anyway, when the Golden Fleece in Pavement and the Old White Swan in Goodramgate each applied for a licence to install one, York's Chief Constable refused, describing them as 'unsuitable and undesirable instruments to have in a public house bar or lounge'. Drinking yourself stupid was fine though. The concern also was that the landlord had no control of the choice of music selected and that a random injudicious choice of record may annoy other customers. On the other hand, record players or radiograms were permitted in five other York pubs, and the Licensing Justices allowed a special case for York Empire in 1959 when the owners sagely pointed out that the absence of a jukebox would drive youngsters onto the streets where hooliganism would surely ensue.

ATRICK COTTER, USUALLY KNOWN AS O'BRIEN, THE IRISH GIANT.
HE STOOD EIGHT FEET THREE INCHES IN HIS STOCKINGS.

THE LAST DROP INN

Colliergate
27 Colliergate, York YO1 8BN
01904 621951
www.York-brewery.co.uk/pubs/last-drop-inn

A York Brewery pub; the others are Mr Foley's Tap House (Leeds); The Tap Room; The Three Legged Mare; Yorkshire Terrier. The Last Drop opened in 2000. Big glass windows look onto King's Square with its myriad street entertainers. The pub is very close to the historic Shambles and the city market.

In 1868 the New Drop replaced the public gallows that had been moved from the Knavesmire in 1801. The New Drop, near the castle, was where the roundabout at St George's car park is today. Roughly opposite, in the museum wall, is a small doorway through which the condemned, including Henry Senior in 1813, were led to the gallows. Senior, aged forty, was hanged, along with Henry Sutcliffe and John Robinson, on Saturday 3 April 1813. Senior's crime was defrauding his creditors – the first man in Yorkshire to swing for this felony. Sutcliffe, twenty-nine, was executed for forgery; Robinson, also forty and a former ship's doctor's mate, then a quack, was hanged for robbing John Naylor, a butcher from Boroughbridge. The last *public* execution was of Frederick Parker in 1868, a convicted murderer: 5,000 people came to gawp. After that, hangings were behind closed doors at the New Drop. The last man to hang in York, the last drop, under the black flag was August Carlsen who was hanged at the New Drop on February 29 1896 for the murder of Julia Wood.

THE DUKE OF YORK

King's Square
3–4 King's Square, York YO1 8BH
01904 676065
www.lbdukeofYork.co.uk

Opened in October 2013, the Duke of York is a Leeds brewery pub. It is a conversion of a former estate agents, split over two floors and close to Shambles.

OLD SHAMBLES TAVERN

Shambles
44 Shambles
York YO1 7LX
01904 633005
www.shamblestavern.co.uk

A café gradually turning into a pub.

Mentioned in the *Domesday* the Latin name for Shambles is *in Macello*. Along with nearby Whipmawhopmagate it is perhaps one of the most famous streets in the world and the most visited street in Europe. In 2010 it won the *Google Britain's Most Picturesque Street Award*. Shambles was originally called Haymongergate to signify the hay that was here to feed the livestock before slaughter; after that, it was called Needlergate after the needles made here from the bones of slaughtered animals. It gets its present name (at first The Great Flesh Shambles) from the fleshammels – a shammel being the wooden board butchers used to display their meat on. They would throw their past-sell-by-date meat, offal, blood and guts into the runnel in the middle of the street to add to the mess caused by routine chamber pot disposal from the overhanging jetties. Now you know what a real shambles really is.

In 1280 seventeen butchers paid an annual shammel toll of seventy shillings between them; in 1872 twenty-five out of the thirty-nine shops here were butchers out of a total of eighty-eight in the whole of York. There were also four pubs: The Globe (closed 1936); The Eagle and Child (closed 1925); The Neptune (closed 1903) and The Shoulder of Mutton (closed 1898). The street is narrow by design, to keep the sun off the meat.

THE GOLDEN LION

Church Street
9 Church Street, York YO1 8BG
01904 620942

The Golden Lion in 2018.

The Golden Lion was originally home to a wealthy local cotton trader and mill owner, and first licensed to sell ale in 1771 when Thomas Hessay borrowed money from Richard Booth, licensee of the Golden Fleece. In 1836 part of Girdlergate was cleared to become Church Street and to give access to Thursday Market (St Sampson's Square) and the business from there.

When William Dent took over in 1872 it was named the Golden Lion Spirit Vaults. In 1971, the year of York's 1,900th anniversary, the pub was virtually rebuilt by J.W. Cameron of West Hartlepool and re-named The 1900th. However in 1983, it reverted to its original name, The Golden Lion, by popular request.

The Golden Lion in 1989.

PIVNI

Patrick Pool
6 Patrick Pool, York, YO1 8BB
01904 635464
www.pivni.co.uk

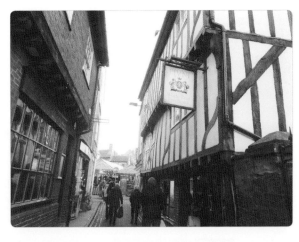

This was the founding bar of the expanding group of Pivovar UK craft beerhouses. This wonderful timber-framed building dates back to 1190; drinking takes place on all three floors.

Pivni means 'beery' in Czech; pivo is 'beer' in Czech, pivnice is a pub. And, in case you need a beer mat, the Czech is 'pivní tácek'. As everyone knows, 'kde jsou toalety?' is Czech for – you guessed it.

St Sampson's Square signs.

THE THREE CRANES

St Sampson's Square
11 St Sampson's Square, York YO1 8RN
01904 653367

The sign on The Three Cranes pub in St Sampson's Square is designed to deceive: the pub is named after the lifting gear used by stallholders rather than anything ornithological. When in December 1874 Robert Halliday left the pub 'in an advanced state of intoxication' he froze to death in the snow. The landlady, Christiana Thompson, was charged with allowing singing and dancing in the pub in 1904 and 1910; the charges were dismissed both times.

THE ROMAN BATH

St Sampson's Square
9 St Sampson's Square, York YO1 8RN
01904 620455

Formerly The Mail Coach, The Barrel Churn (from 1785), The Barrel (from 1818), The Cooper, The Coach & Horses (from 1828), and the Mail Coach (from 1834), the pub is now named after the Roman bathhouse excavated here in 1930 and which is partly visible in a fine museum downstairs, including cold room: *frigidarium,* hot room: *caldarium* and underfloor central heating system: *hypocaust.* Tiles stamped *Legio VI* and *Legio IX* have been uncovered recording legions that were stationed at *Eboracum.*

Two views of the museum under the pub.

THE BURNS HOTEL

Market Street
23 Market St, York YO1 8SL
01904 636962

Until 2013 it was The Hansom Cab. Joseph Aloysius Hansom (1842–1900), the architect and inventor of the Patent Safety Cabriolet that bears his name, was born at 114 Micklegate and christened in the Bar Convent chapel. He suffered from severe depression and shot himself in his office on 27 May 1900. The pub in Market Street named after him was a substantial rebuild in 1975 in the style of the cabs invented by Hansom; Victorian-style panelling, glass (including skylight feature) and lighting lend the pub character. Architecturally, Hansom's best known work is probably the majestic neoclassical Birmingham Town Hall. The Hansom Cab was so common a sight that Disraeli called it 'the gondola of London'.

The pub has recently been renamed The Burns Hotel – one of its former names when it was in what was then Jubbergate. This goes back to a Scot, William McClaren, who was the licensee of the Burns Coffee House in 1838 which had its own brewery. By 1895 it was the Burns Inn. It is a shame that a name with such important associations with York has been replaced.

The Burns Hotel when it was Hansom Cab.

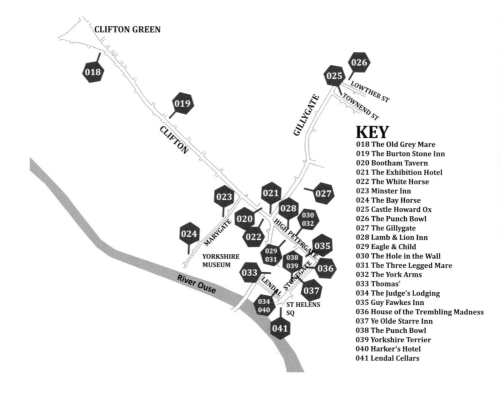

BOOTHAM BAR

Bootham, originally Buthum, means 'at the booths' and signifies the markets that used to be held here; it stands on the northwestern gateway of the Roman fortress and was originally called Galmanlith. A door knocker was added to the Bar in 1501 for the use of Scotsmen (and others, presumably) seeking admission to the city. The barbican came down in 1831 and the wall steps went up in 1889; a statue of Ebrauk, the pre-Roman founder of York, once stood nearby. On the orders of Henry IV Thomas de Mowbray's severed head was stuck here in 1405 and the Earl of Manchester bombarded the Bar in 1644 during the Civil War.

The removal of the barbican was due in part to complaints

Looking through the Bar with the Lamb & Lion and Hole in the Wall on the left.

by residents of Clifton: 'not fit for any female of respectability to pass through' on account of the droppings of animals *en route* to the cattle market and its use as a urinal by pedestrians. Not much change there, then. The three statues on the top were carved in 1894 and feature a mediaeval mayor, a mason and a knight; the mason is holding a model of the restored Bar.

THE OLD GREY MARE

Clifton
Clifton Green, Clifton, York, YO30 6LH
01904 654485
www.oldgreymare.com

The Old Grey Mare is a former coaching Inn dating back to the 17th century.

THE BURTON STONE INN

Clifton
34 Clifton, York YO30 6AW
01904 655715
www.burtonstone.co.uk

This is opposite St Peter's School, one of England's three oldest and *alma mater* of terrorist Guy Fawkes and Marxist historian Christopher Hill. The boundary cross base in front of the pub with its three holes may have been a rallying point for soldiers before going off to war, or it may be a plague stone. Its holes would either have held a cross or have been filled with vinegar and coins deposited: the money allowed those quarantined beyond to buy food; the vinegar acted as a disinfectant. It used to be called The Plough.

For York, jazz, started off properly in the 50s at the York Jazz Club in the dance studios in High Ousegate, later becoming the Studio Club. In 1958 the Jazz Attic Club opened on the top floor of a house in Petergate above Pete Madden's restaurant. In 1955 nine local schoolboys formed a band but had to remain anonymous in the press as their school was anti-group and considered jazz 'unsuitable'. The Empire Jazz club opened in 1959. Jazz could also be heard in the Clifton Ballroom and nearby at the Burton Stone Inn. In 1963 the York Jazz Scene was opened in Acomb Church Hall. Bobby Hirst organised a significant concert of modern jazz in the Tempest Anderson Hall at the Yorkshire Museum followed in 1966 by another big jazz concert in St George's Hall.

The pub in the 1920s.

The boundary cross base today.

BOOTHAM TAVERN

Bootham
29 Bootham, York, YO30 7BW
01904 620251
www.boothamtavernYork.co.uk

THE EXHIBITION HOTEL

Bootham
19 Bootham, York YO30 7BW
01904 641105

The hotel gets its name from the 1879 *Yorkshire Fine Art and Industrial Exhibition* that took place nearby. It is the product of much demolition: the 18th century Bird in Hand next to Bootham Bar was demolished when the Bar's barbican was torn down. It was rebuilt over the road on the corner of Bootham and St Leonard's but that too came down when Exhibition Square was built. It moved into an 18th century town house where the Exhibition is now and took the current name. Despite this, it was sometimes referred to as Churchill's hotel after a landlord. When Henry Dyson took over (he had owned Scawin's Railway Hotel) he changed the name to Dyson's Family and Commercial Hotel but it soon reverted to the Exhibition.

A temporary building was erected in the grounds of Bootham Park Hospital for the first Exhibition. Made entirely from wood and glass the front was decorated with Royal coats of arms and those of the patrons. The Italianate building opened its doors to the public in 1879 for the second *Exhibition*, inspired by the Great Exhibition in London of 1851. The York exhibition attracted more than half a million visitors and made a profit of £12,000. In 1892 it became the City Art Gallery. The building continued in use from 1880 as the Yorkshire Fine Art and Industrial Institution until 1892 when it was purchased by the City Council. The original building had a 'Great Exhibition Hall' at the rear with room for 2,000 people. This was a venue for boxing and cock fighting as well as exhibitions; it was damaged by bombs during World War II and demolished in 1942.

THE WHITE HORSE

Bootham
6 Bootham, York YO30 7BL
01904 628700
www.thewhitehorseYork.co.uk

MINSTER INN

Marygate
24 Marygate, York YO30 7BH
01904 849240
www.minsterinn.co.uk

The Minster Inn was opened in 1903 by Tadcaster Tower Brewery to replace a previous pub recorded first in 1823 on the opposite side of the road, against the walls of the grounds of St Mary's Abbey. Around that time it was called the York Minster but changed its name to the Gardner's Arms in 1851. Beatrice Palmer lived in the new pub with her landlady mother and sister; unfortunately, she collapsed and died in the De Grey Rooms during the 1951 election results.

THE BAY HORSE

68 Marygate, York YO30 7BH
01904 541926
www.bayhorsemarygate.co.uk

The Bay Horse was originally in the gatehouse to St Mary's Abbey opposite, but obliged to vacate when the gatehouse was required for the keeper of the Yorkshire Philosophical Society's Museum in 1839. A new pub was built against the abbey walls only to be demolished in 1893. In 1896 it was rebuilt over the road. There was a bottle and jug department on the ground floor. Currently closed

The original Bay Horse in 1897.

CASTLE HOWARD OX

Townend Street
The Groves, York YO31 7QA
01904 622791

The name comes from an ox called White Willy, owned by a syndicate the members of which lived near Castle Howard; White Willy was exhibited in York in 1833. The pub was opened in 1836 by William Lund who obtained a licence to open a house on Bootham Stray, which begins at Townend Street.

THE PUNCH BOWL

Lowther Street
134 Lowther St, York YO31 7ND
01904 624549

One of three surviving Punch Bowls in York, the other two being in Stonegate and Blossom Street. This one was recently called the Independent but reverted to its original name. The licensee during the 1940s and 50s was Mel Rosser, ex-Wales, England and GB rugby player: the pub was locally referred to as Rosser's rather than the Punch Bowl.

THE GILLYGATE

Gillygate
48 Gillygate, York YO31 7EQ
01904 654103
www.gillygateYork.co.uk

The Gillygate started serving in 1811 as the Waggon & Horses. In 1902 it boasted a Lady's Market Room, just for women. In 2003 it became the Gillygate. Gillygate the street gets its name from St Giles Church, which was demolished after 1547. The street was cleared in 1644 and rebuilt for the most part in the late eighteenth and early nineteenth centuries.

LAMB & LION INN

High Petergate
2-4 High Petergate
York YO1 7EH
01904 612078
www.lambandlionYork.com

Right under the bar.

EAGLE & CHILD

High Petergate
9 High Petergate, York YO1 7EN
01904 631536
info@eagleandchildYork.co.uk

Built in 1640, the Grade II* listed timber-framed pub is a Leeds Brewery house converted in November 2015 from the building previously occupied by Plunkets restaurant since 1977. The building is reputed to have once been owned by the Terry family of chocolate fame and is famous for the graffiti scrawled on the upstairs bar wall in lipstick by the five original members of the Rolling Stones when it was a coffee bar called Pete Maddens; the Stones were in there after a concert in Leeds in 1968. The autographed wall has been preserved for posterity.

There was a pub of the same name in Shambles, but the most famous Eagle & Child is the one in St Giles, Oxford. The name derives from the crest of the Earl of Derby; the image refers to a story of a high-born baby found in an eagle's nest. All such named pubs have the nickname 'Bird and Baby', or the less delicate 'Fowl and Foetus'.

The 'Rolling Stones Room'.

THE HOLE IN THE WALL

High Petergate

10 High Petergate
York YO1 7EH
01904 634468
www.holeinthewallYork.co.uk

Wolstenholme's Dram Shop led the way from 1869; when Thomas Blakey Haigh took over in 1887 he renamed it Haigh's Vaults; German brewed lagers and pilsner beers were available even then. 1902 saw a relocation and a new name: the Petergate Wine & Spirit Stores & Bar. This lasted until 1953 when it became the Board. The building was deemed dangerous and renovated, re-opening in 1981 as The Hole in the Wall.

Another Hole in the Wall may have been open nearby in earlier days. By 1351 the Archbishop of York could boast a prison — the 'bishop prison' or 'convict prison' for criminal clerks and those who had successfully 'pleaded clergy'; it was in the archbishop's palace in 1385 probably in the crypt below St Sepulchre's Chapel. When the chapel, which had been converted into a public house, The Hole in the Wall, was demolished in 1816, a prison was discovered beneath it. This public house had been named after a cavity, apparently in the wall of the prison, which was thought to have been used for

The Hole in the Wall from the upper window of the Eagle & Child.

walling up prisoners, but Hargrove shows that it was an entrance to the prison.

The former Hole in Wall public house was built adjacent to the northwest corner of minster. St Sepulchre's Chapel was here along with and the main gateway into the grounds of the Old Archbishop's Palace. It was demolished in 1816 at the same time as the nearby St Peter's Prison.

Morris Dancers (not) in the Bar in January 2018.

THE THREE LEGGED MARE

High Petergate
15 High Petergate, York YO1 7EN
01904 638246
www.threeleggedmareYork.co.uk

This York Brewery pub is named after a triangular type of industrial gallows which despatched three felons at once; one was in use at the Knavesmire until 1801 before it was removed in 1812. There is a replica of the fearsome 'wonkey donkey' in the beer garden of the pub – the salutary lesson to be learned is that there is absolutely no future in riding the three legged mare.

The pub is owned by the York Brewery, which started brewing in 1996 – the first local brewers to emerge since the closure of Aldwark-based Hunt's in 1956. The brewery's other York pubs are The Last Drop Inn in Colliergate; The Yorkshire Terrier in Stonegate and The Tap Room in the brewery itself in Toft Green.

York's Tyburn gallows had been on the Knavesmire from 1379, the name a chilling reminder of London's notorious Tyburn. Public executions became a very popular feature of a day at the races. The last hanging there was in 1801 – Edward Hughes was the convict, guilty of rape – after which the gallows were moved to the New Drop near the castle. A paved area with a small plaque today marks where the Tyburn scaffold was – on Tadcaster Road, opposite Pulleyn Drive. It was originally a gibbet post; the gallows replaced the gibbet in 1379 and remained until finally pulled down in 1812.

Other York gallows were at Gallows Close in Burton Stone Lane under the jurisdiction of the abbot of St Mary's Abbey and first recorded in 1444–1445, demolished by 1802; and at the Horse Fair at White Cross Hill near the present junction of Haxby and Wigginton roads. It was first used in 1690, and was rebuilt in 1693. There were gallows on Foss Bridge administered by the Archbishop of York and those owned by St Leonard's Hospital on Green Dykes, now Garrow Hill, and close to Thief Lane along which convicted robbers were led to the scaffold. It is recorded in use from 1374–1375 until 1444–1445, and redundant by 1500 but in use again in 1571 until 1676. It was dismantled in 1700. A gallows belonging to Holy Trinity existed between 1150-4 and there was a gallows in the Hull Road, at Gallows Hole, which was abandoned by 1693.

When a crime was committed inside a house, temporary gallows might be erected to hang the criminal at the front door. For cases involving multiple offenders, multiple temporary gallows were erected, with one noose per condemned criminal. In one case we know of a condemned man suffered an agonising strangulation for forty minutes until he finally died from asphyxiation.

The famous Tyburn gallows in London – where Marble Arch is now – was triangular, with three uprights and three crossbeams, allowing up to twenty-four men and women to be executed simultaneously. In later years, a scaffold with a trap door was used throughout Britain, through which victims dropped and, in theory, died quickly from a broken neck rather than through strangulation, especially when weights were fixed to their ankles. Public executions came to an end in 1868, after which hangings were conducted within prison walls in private.

THE YORK ARMS

High Petergate
26 High Petergate, York YO1 7EH
01904 624508

Over the street, on the site of the Peter Prison. From 1733 it was Carr's Coffee House, then from 1789 the Chapter Coffee House when John Kilby – a brewer and Lord Mayor, took it on, then The Eclipse in 1818, The Board after an 1838 rebuild, back to The Chapter Coffee House in 1843 and The York Arms in 1860. The derivation of the Eclipse is the name of an unbeaten racehorse owned by the Duke of Cumberland who named it after the eclipse of 1764, the year in which the horse was born.

The pub is named after the city's coat of arms. The earliest records of York's Coat of Arms are in the Corporation minutes of 1 February 1587, which tell us that the Lord Mayor received the Coat of Arms of the City, on parchment, from the Queen's Herald of Arms. The common features are the red cross of St George, reflecting the city's ecclesiastical importance connections, and the five gold lions of England, underlying its Royalist leanings. The lions are 'passant' (walking) and 'guardant' (facing the viewer): they are, therefore, active and alert. The civic sword and mace show the city's powers of self-government under the mayor; the sword was presented to the city by Richard II in 1387; he thus allowed it to be carried before the mayor on ceremonial occasions; a charter in 1396 allowed a similar right for the mace.

The Rolling Stones were not the only band to grace High Petergate. In May 1985 the Clash followed them, coming to York as part of that legendary busking tour that they undertook with no money in their pockets, relying on just what they took in the hat to pay for transport, board and lodge. St Sampson's Square was their pitch of choice while the York Arms was their pub of choice; here, they performed an impromptu concert to the delight of a growing throng of fans.

THOMAS'S

Museum Street
3 Museum St, York YO1 7DT
01904 637901
www.thomasofYorkpubandkitchenYork.com

The pediment.

Thomas's dates from around 1861 when hotelier William Thomas bought the site, which had hitherto been the site of Etridge's Royal Hotel – royal because King Christian VII of Denmark stayed there in 1768, as did George, Prince of Wales in 1788. Etridge was a prominent Whig, and his hotel was where the York Whig Club was formed. In 1876 Thomas sold his pub to Thomas Lightfoot, a brewer from Bedale.

The doorway boasts a colourful relief sculpture depicting a court jester with bauble and a well dressed Sir Walter Raleigh-type figure with tankard and pipe. What does it tell us? That this is the place to come for a drink, a smoke and a good laugh. Smoke no more.

Thomas's was popular with actors and theatre-goers, as it is so close to the Theatre Royal. It was in 1744 that the first playhouse was built on the site of the present theatre.

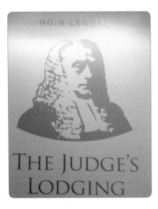

THE JUDGE'S LODGING

Lendal
9 Lendal, York, YO1 8AQ
01904 638733
www.judgeslodgingYork.co.uk

This Thwaites pub is situated in the original cellars of the Assize Court Judge's Lodgings, accommodating drinkers in the numerous nooks. The Judge's Lodging is a Grade I listed Georgian townhouse and was a good place to stay for the judiciary attending the assizes, convenient as it was for the Assembly Rooms (over the road) and Terry's Restaurant (round the corner), from which breakfasts were delivered to our learned friends each morning.

The Lodgings is on the site of a late Roman interval tower and was built in 1726 for Dr Wintringham (d. 1748), a very eminent doctor and physician at York County Hospital in 1746. An effigy of Aesculapius, Graeco-Roman god of medicine and health, guards the door. Wintringham has a monument in his memory at Westminster Abbey; he is buried in St Michael-le-Belfrey next to the Minster. When the Judges were in residence they took an official breakfast on day one at the Mansion House as guests of the Lord Mayor, to which they would process in their wigs and robes. It was the official judges' residence until 1976.

GUY FAWKES INN

High Petergate
25 High Petergate, York YO1 7HP
01904 623716
www.guyfawkesinnYork.com

This 1707 pub is a celebration of one of England's most notorious traitors and treasonists, a would-be mass murderer, and a 17th century radicalised terrorist. Real gas lights and candles still flicker in the public rooms here, adding

Sculptures on the backyard wall.

to the conspiratorial atmosphere. A window from 1801 at the top of a staircase shows the arms of York and the House of Hanover. In 1905 the building was recorded as Wasling's Boarding Hotel. When Charles Henry Young took over in the 1920s he renamed it Young's Hotel.

Fawkes was born just off nearby Stonegate, not in the pub, baptised at St Michael le Belfry (opposite the pub) and was a pupil at St Peter's, now up the road in Clifton. When he grew up Fawkes inherited property in York, at Gillygate and Clifton; on his 21st birthday he sold his estate and enlisted in the Catholic Spanish army. As Captain Guido Fawkes he pursued a distinguished military record, and his expertise with explosives led the plotters to recruit him in their attempt to assassinate James I and replace him with a Catholic monarch. Guy Fawkes, calling himself Johnson, a servant to Thomas Percy, smuggled thirty-six barrels of gunpowder under the

The famous window in the hotel part of the pub.

The plotters' mural in the yard.

House of Lords, ready for its royal opening on 5 November 1605. Fawkes was on guard; it was his job to light the fuse, then head to Flanders to raise forces who would join in the Catholic uprising in England. Just before midnight he was arrested, 'booted and spurred', ready to make his get-away, having on his person a watch, lantern, tinder-box and slow fuses. He was interviewed by King James in his bedchamber, taken to the Tower to be tortured, and finally 'hanged, drawn and quartered' as a traitor on 31 January 1606. Though he is still commonly burnt in effigy on 5 November ('Plot Night' as it is called in parts of Yorkshire) no Guy, or should that be Guido?, is ever burnt at St Peter's.

HOUSE OF THE TREMBLING MADNESS

48 Stonegate, York YO1 8AS
01904 640009
www.tremblingmadness.co.uk

Great bar, great décor, great beer shop. The website blurb is more eloquent than I could ever be …

the trembling madness….or delirium tremens (DTs) as it's more commonly known has been around since people have been drinking that intoxicating liquor. And our medieval hall has lived through times of hardship and experienced much death. The rear end started life in 1180 ad as the first Norman House to be built in York and still that wall holds up the old ship beams above our heads, those beams sailed the seas over 800 years ago. Our friends' heads upon the walls look out across over a century of being hunted and killed. We value our history and have learnt from our ancestors to enjoy ourselves as they did by feeding and watering ourselves frequently in this tavern. The Trembling Madness may eventually get us and there's still room for a few more heads upon the wall. Thank you Yorkshire for your feast of wondrous food and beer. Time to enjoy and time to live the madness way …

Some random wildlife on the walls here.

At time of writing the trembling madness was rumoured to be spreading to Lendal …

YE OLDE STARRE INN

Stonegate
40 Stonegate, York YO1 8AS
01904 623063
www.York-wiki.co.uk/ye-olde-starre-inne-York.html

This is York's oldest licensed public house, serving us since at least 1644. The earliest reference is of a printer, Puritan sympathiser Thomas Broad, dwelling at Mistress Roger's house in Stonegate, 'over against the Starre' in 1644.

Some say the pub is named after Charles I – popularly known as 'the Old Star'; we do know for sure that it was used as a Civil War morgue, field station and operating theatre by the Parliamentarians, much to the disgust of the Royalist landlord, William Foster. Others say it is a reference to the Star of Bethlehem guiding pilgrims along Stonegate to the Minster (and pub!). Others still connect it with the sixteen-pointed star that is the badge of the Worshipful Company of Innholders. The cellar is 10th century and the well was once the only source of clean water in the area.

The main block at the back of the yard is mid-16th century; the left hand block is c.1600. Originally, there was a coaching yard in front, but with the coming of the railways in 1840 this became redundant, and the yard was infilled with a shop fronting Stonegate, hence the present long passage to the pub. It was this boxing in that affected trade and inspired landlord Thomas Bulman in 1733 to erect the striking gallows sign of the Olde Starre Inne which still stretches impressively across the street – to advertise the pub. He made a contract with neighbours John Moore, a shoemaker, and George Ambler, a saddler, allowing him to fix his sign to their premises across Stonegate; he was to pay them 5/- each at Candlemas, but with the clever proviso that they had to spent the fee in his company (i.e. in his pub!). In 1886 the sign read 'Boddy's Star Inn' after landlord William Horner Boddy, who previously ran the Navigation Tavern in Skeldergate.

The Starre had stabling behind used as stabling for circus and theatrical parties from the Theatre Royal, so the pub was popular with actors. Ye Old Starre was sold for £250 in 1662, and in 1683 it was inherited by Edward Thompson, grandfather of General Wolfe, who also owned the Old Black Swan, Peasholme Green. Until 1923 the pub was plain Star Inn. Another name was Turf Coffee House.

THE PUNCH BOWL

Stonegate
7 Stonegate, York YO1 8AN
01904 655147
www.http://York-wiki.co.uk/
punchbowl-stonegate-York.html

The Punch Bowl, like the pubs of the same name in Blossom Street and Lowther Street, is indicative of the vogue for drinking punch from the end of the 17th century. As a new, fashionable drink it caught on amongst the Whigs, leading to the sign of the punchbowl denoting inns patronised by Whigs. The Tories, ever conservative, stuck with their predilection for red wines and port.

The pub has a close association with the Minster bell ringers. In 1729 the Society of York Scholars was formed. After 1765 the society changed their name to the Society of St Peter's Youths. Around the same time the ring of bells at the Minster was being replaced: coincidentally, the Punch Bowl Inn Stonegate was refitting a window in its back room – the Copper Bar. This left one of the main beams unsupported, so the ringers brought in the discarded tenor bell clapper to carry the weight. The clapper can still be seen in the bar to this day; the pub remains the preferred oasis for the ringers as well.

1831 was a bad year, for it was then that the pub put three albino children on display for the people of York to gawp at for the sum of 6d. The following year was not much better: that was when a mob of Tories broke into the pub demanding redress for alleged voting irregularities by the Whigs. In 1856 York Brotherly Society held their centenary dinner here, while in 1860 the pub hosted the Kingston Unity of Oddfellows. In 1880 landlord William Hanforth was charged and fined for keeping 'a disorderly house' with twenty-four 'immoral' people living there.

The Punch Bowl is also the place where the Gimcrack Club held their annual lunches, at which the winner of the Gimcrack Stakes run on the Knavesmire was obliged to supply three bottles of champagne to mark the occasion.

The striking and beautiful façade is not Tudor; it went up in 1931 after a refurbishment following a fire. Hospitality here began with a coffee house dating from 1675. It was licensed as a pub in 1671 and known as the Golden Punch Bowl.

YORKSHIRE TERRIER

Stonegate
10 Stonegate, York YO1 8AS
01904 676711
www.YorkshireterrierYork.co.uk

This pub has also a stunning façade, visible when you look up from the entrance to the Punch Bowl across the street. The Yorkshire Terrier pub first opened its doors in 2004.

Stonegate is by common consent one of the finest streets in England, if not Europe, and York's first 'foot-street'. It was pedestrianised in 1971 and paved the way for many more. The old Roman stone paving – hence the name – survives under the cobbles complete with the central gulley for the chariots' skid wheels. It was the Roman *Via Praetoria*. Stonegate was once famous for its coffee shops (hence Coffee Yard).

By the early 19th century there was a wide range of shops, including the apothecary of a Mr Palmer, Mrs Hopton's where corsets might be purchased, and Thomas Hardy's, which sold gentlemen's breeches. Stonegate can boast a long line of York booksellers stretching back to Francis Hildyard's shop established 'at the sign of The Bible, Stonegate' in 1682. In 1763 this became John Todd and Henry Sotheran until 1774 when Sotheran set up on his own next to St Helen's church soon moving across the Square to where the Savings Bank was. Henry Cave's late 18th century Todd's Book and Print Warehouse, as with many booksellers of the time, was something of an apothecary too, with a popular line in rat poison, negus and lemonade and similar preparations and confections. Roman busts watched over the 30,000 or so books. John Wolstenholme sold books in nearby Minster Gates, his building graced by his brother's fine statue of Minerva. Other evidence for this bookish aspect of York society are the red Printer's Devil and Coffee Yard off Stonegate.

Thomas Godfrey was a phrenologist who invented his qualifications; he opened his first bookshop at 46½ Stonegate in 1895 selling second hand books 'recently purchased from private libraries'. The business was imaginatively called 'Ye Olde Boke Shoppe' but it failed: Godfrey 'became dissatisfied of the apathy of the citizens and disposed of the business' – sentiments and actions that could be echoed by many an independent bookseller today. An alternative report, though, attributes his failure to the selling of Oscar Wilde's *Portrait of Dorian Gray* after it had been recalled by the publishers, thus giving 'offence to some of the good people in York by his handling of a book which was regarded at the time as a most indecent publication'. Godfrey tried again in 1904 at 37 Goodramgate with the Eclectic Book Company, eventually moving back to 16 Stonegate with a business just as imaginatively named The Book Company, later Edward S. Pickard. In 1982 the business moved over the road to 32 Stonegate and acquired a second shop on the campus at York University.

The 'Printer's Devil' effigy at 33 Stonegate at the corner of Coffee Yard has been looking down on us there since the 1880s and signifies the importance and prevalence of the printing, bookselling and publishing industries in the area. A printer's devil was a printer's apprentice, a factotum. Printing was commonly known as 'the black art' on account of the inks. The Devil is indicative of the common practice of denoting one's trade with a symbol – other examples are at 74a Petergate: the wonderful cigar shop Native American Indian complete with headdress from around 1800, and, as noted, the Minerva, at the corner of Minster Gates indicating a bookseller. The reason for all this symbolism was simply that, at the time, most people could not read: even by 1870 one in three York women and one in five men could neither read nor write – so written signs were often useless; the practice declined somewhat from 1760 when signs were outlawed and house numbering and literacy increased.

Medieval action outside Harker's.

HARKER'S HOTEL

1 St Helen's Square, York YO1 8QN
01904 672795

Built on the site of The York Tavern in 1770, a coaching house with room for 150 horses. Harker's was named after a butler who had worked at The Tavern. It was pulled down in 1928 so that St Helen's Square could be widened (it used to be triangular). Harker's then decamped to Dringhouses; a 1929 advertisement claimed it to be 'The best and most up to date hotel in the city'.

The name lives on in the Square though: Harker's Bar now occupies the grand Yorkshire Insurance Company building, which opened in 1924.

LENDAL CELLARS

Lendal
26 Lendal, York, YO1 8AA
01904 623121

Lendal Cellars opened in 1984 and consists of a group of brick-built buildings constructed in the 18th and 19th centuries and is right next to the recently restored Mansion House, the residence of the Lord Major of York. This historic pub is located under three large brick arches, which were originally the Lord Mayor's wine cellars in a brick-vaulted semi-basement.

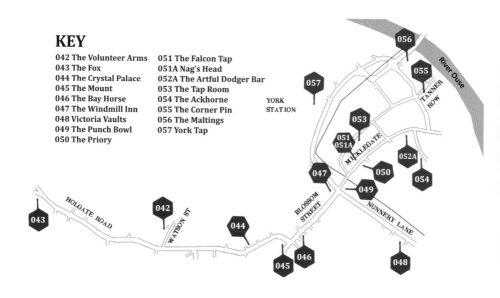

MICKLEGATE BAR

Micklegate Bar was originally called Mickleith, which means 'great gate'; the royal arms resplendent on the Bar are those of Edward III; the arch is Norman; the rest 14th century; the side arch was added in 1753. Being on the road to and from London, this was the Bar through which royal visitors entered York. Edward IV, Richard III, Henry VII, Margaret Tudor, James I, Charles I (on three Civil War occasions) and James II all passed through. Henry VIII was scheduled to enter here but, in the event, came in through Walmgate Bar. Heads and bloody quarters of traitors were routinely displayed on the top, most famously: Lord Scrope of Mastan in 1415; Sir Henry Percy (Hotspur) after his part in the rebellion against Henry IV; Richard Duke of York after the Battle of Wakefield in 1460, prompting Shakespeare to write: 'Off with his head and set it on York's gates; so York did overlook the town of York' (Queen Margaret in *Henry VI*); Thomas Percy in 1569 – his head remained rotting there for two years. Removal of heads without permission was, not inappropriately, punishable by beheading – guess where the heads ended up. The last grisly displays were in 1746 after the Jacobite Rebellion at Culloden. Duke 'Butcher' Cumberland on his victorious return from bloody Culloden left a number of prisoners here to show his gratitude for the city's hospitality: the Sheriff's chaplain read out the message: 'And the Lord said unto Moses "Take all the heads of the people and hang them up before the sun".' Twenty-three were duly left to hang for ten minutes, stripped and quartered, their heads stuck on the Bar. The heads of James Mayne and William Connelly remained on the Bar until 1754. The barbican was removed in 1826 to allow a circus access to the city; the east side arch was built in 1827.

THE VOLUNTEER ARMS

Watson Street
5 Watson St, York YO24 4BH
01904 541945
www.volunteerarmsYork.co.uk

The Volunteer Arms dates back at least 144 years; The Locomotive, which was next door to The Volunteer Arms, closed recently after 159 years of trade, the land used for houses.

THE FOX

Holgate
169 Holgate Road, Holgate, York, YO24 4DQ
01904 787722
www.ossett-brewery.co.uk/pubs/fox-York

Home of York's largest beer garden, The Fox Inn dates from 1878, still retains its original compartmented room layout, and is Grade II listed. The pub, obviously, was a watering hole for the carriage works workers nearby before they closed. At its height, the works employed 5,000 people across a 45-acre site.

THE CRYSTAL PALACE

Holgate
66–68 Holgate, York, YO24 4AB
01904 625305

The Crystal Palace has been going since 1851. It looks like a house, but it really is a pub. It is named after The Crystal Palace Exhibition, rather than the football team of the same name. The actual Crystal Palace was a cast-iron and magnificent plate-glass building in London's Hyde Park to house the Great Exhibition of 1851. More than 14,000 exhibitors from all over the world gathered in the 92,000 m2 exhibition area to display examples of technology developed in the Industrial Revolution. The Great Exhibition building was 1,851 feet long, with an interior height of 128 feet. It was three times the size of St Paul's Cathedral.

THE MOUNT

The Mount
72 The Mount, York, YO24 1AR
01904 289740

The 1832 Mount public house was called the Saddle until John Smith bought it in 1892; the current pub has a fine sign depicting a mounted cavalryman.

THE BAY HORSE

Blossom Street
55 Blossom Street, York, YO24 1AZ
(01904) 654998
www.York-pubs.co.uk/thebayhorse

The Bay Horse is a 17th century pub with unspoilt interior: sloping floors, big beams and original fireplaces make this a traditional English pub that also had a brewhouse. The Bay Horse dates back more than 265 years, and occupies a key spot on one of the busiest routes into the city centre. Controversy rages over whether this Bay Horse or The Bay Horse (now Keystones) in Monkgate were once called The Bay Malton, named after a horse which flourished between 1764 and 1767.

In 1861 Richard Cowper, professional horse breaker, was licensee; he sold out to the Institute of the Blessed Virgin Mary.

Visit www.black-horse-pub.com for Joe Bratton's theory on the origin of this name.

I became curious about the inn sign 'The Bay Horse'. On the face of it, it is just another recognised colour of a horse. This being the case it might be expected to be, more or less, evenly distributed around the country … but it is not. Apart from 5 isolated Southern examples, Bay Horse pubs are found only in the North, predominently Yorkshire but also Lancashire, Northumberland/Durham and a few in Scotland. What's more they are found in clusters … York has a confusing number of Bay Horses and in Felling there are two so close together they are identified as the Top Bay Horse and the Bottom Bay Horse. My theory is that the bay horse in the inn sign is not a generic brown coloured horse but a Cleveland Bay, a specific breed of horse emanating from the Cleveland area of North East England. In the Cleveland area itself … Middlesborough [sic] and surrounding towns there are a few pubs actually called 'Cleveland Bay' It is Britain's oldest breed of horse. (Throughout the middle ages the Monastic houses in the North East were the principal breeders of pack horses. The ancestors of today's Cleveland Bays, particularly on the female side, were such pack horses bred in the Yorkshire Dales).

THE WINDMILL INN

Blossom Street
14–16 Blossom St, York YO24 1AJ
01904 238235

The Windmill, complete with brew house, has kept growing since the late 18th century; it is first recorded in 1769. Apparently, it gets its name because from the pub you could see Nun Mill on Bishopthorpe Road and two windmills on the Mount.

St Michael once appeared here on a white horse before drinkers, on his way to protect the nuns at the Bar Convent over the road from an anti-Catholic mob. A sign once read: 'Good entertainment for all that passes – Horses, mares, men and asses.'

The hotel in 1920.

VICTORIA VAULTS

Nunnery Lane
47–49 Nunnery Lane, York YO23 1AB
01904 654307
www.victoriavaults.com

Regular live music is the keynote of this pub.

THE PUNCH BOWL

Blossom Street
5–9 Blossom Street, York, YO24 1AU
01904 666740

The pub on the right in 1962.

The pub from the Windmill in September 2017.

St Thomas's Hospital was next to Micklegate Bar but was demolished in 1862. In 1851 it was an almshouse 'for aged widows' taking in permanent residents and travellers for food and lodging. Until 1791 these widows had to beg on the streets for four days every year for their alms. The 1770 Punch Bowl stands on the site now, indicative, like the pubs of the same name in Stonegate and Leeman Road, of the Whiggish vogue for drinking punch from the end of the seventeenth century. As a new, fashionable drink it caught on amongst the Whigs leading to the sign of the punchbowl denoting inns patronised by Whigs.

THE PRIORY

Micklegate
103 Micklegate, York YO1 6LB
01904 653231

In 1089 Benedictine monks from the Abbey of St Martin of Marmoutier near Tours, the 'Alien Benedictines', established a priory here on the site of a pre-Conquest church, itself possibly the successor of Alcuin of York's great Saxon church, the Alma Sophia. 'Aliens', because they were just that. Not surprisingly, being an alien house, Holy Trinity suffered local prejudice during the various wars with France. The monks were suspected of granting asylum to French spies; they were charged with supplying the enemy and there was frequent unrest at the priory as a consequence. During the reign of Henry VI (1422–1461) the priory received the grant of another religious house, the hospital of St Nicholas in Lawrence Street.

At the Dissolution of the Monasteries charges of sodomy, sexual incontinence and superstition were brought against the prior and his brethren. The prior evidently took some part in the Pilgrimage of Grace in 1536; in 1538 he and his ten brother priests surrendered the house.

Part of the priory was converted into tenements and 'ruthlessly demolished … a monument of the ancient grandeur of our venerable city'. In 1854 the gateway to the priory was knocked down to make way for the building of Priory Street. Apart from the Priory Church of Holy Trinity, down the road, all that is sadly left as a reminder is the Priory pub, formerly the Coach & Horses in 1818; in 1945 Tetley's refurbished it and called it the Coach and the Little Coach until 1996 when it was the Phalanx & Firkin. From 2003 it has been the Priory.

The pub's relative proximity to the railways has served it well. In 1867 engine men met there to discuss strike action; in 1875 The National Federation of Enginemen's Protection Association held their annual conference there; signalmen convened there in 1892 to discuss pay and hours. In 1902 the Chief Constable insisted that the ad hoc toilet located down a narrow passage be replaced with permanent facilities.

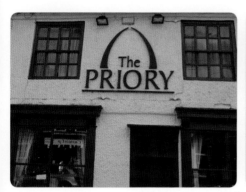 

Priory old and new with Bar in the background.

THE FALCON TAP

Micklegate
94 Micklegate, York YO1 6JX
(01904) 622225
www.thefalcontap.co.uk

Originally just the Falcon, dating from 1770s, it was also called Rumours in 2002. It has now refurbished and renamed the Falcon Tap. In 1736, York historian Francis Drake named it as one of only two noteworthy inns in Micklegate. In 1818, no less an authority than William Hargrove described it as a 'very excellent inn' and the only one of consequence in Micklegate. And in a 1902 survey the Chief Constable found this one pub worthy of praise. The wooden falcon placed above the frontage in 1880 survives. In 1842 the pub was demolished and rebuilt.

NAG'S HEAD

Micklegate
100 Micklegate, York YO1 6JX
01904 622492

This was formerly the Nag's Head, then Sociale in 2016 and now Nag's Head again from 2017. The nag's head must be spinning.

THE ARTFUL DODGER BAR

Micklegate
47 Micklegate, York YO1 6LJ
01904 644102

Scenes from Dickens' *Oliver Twist* adorn the walls in keeping with the name of the pub. It was formerly Walker's Bar, named after Mrs Walker who was the patron of this and the nightclub next door.

THE TAP ROOM

Toft Green
12 Toft Green, York, YO1 6JT
01904 621162
www.York-brewery.co.uk/Pubs/The-Tap-Room

The York Brewery website puts it best:

> The Brewery Tap Room has a unique atmosphere to sit back, relax and enjoy a pint of award-winning York Beer … the brewery taproom bar is nestled inside the brewery itself up on Toft Green. Enjoy the smells drifting from the brewery whilst reading the newspaper and enjoying a pint of cask ale.

THE ACKHORNE

St Martin's Lane
9 St Martin's Lane, York YO1 6LR
01904 671421
www.York-pubs.co.uk/theackhorne

This is a fine 18th century traditional pub in a cobbled street off Micklegate. John Hill, owner of the Golden Ball, bought the premises in 1738 and converted what was then a house into the pub. In 1818 it was known as the Acorn but reverted to the original name in 1993. It had a dram shop but the toilets were shared by the family and the customers. In 1884 it was bought by brewers Hotham & Co., later Tower Brewery, Tadcaster. Camerons of West Hartlepool (now Hartlepool) bought it in 1961.

The Ackhorne when it was just The Acorn about 1989.

THE CORNER PIN

Tanner Row
17 Tanner Row, York, YO1 6JB
01904 629946

The Corner Pin is a 400-year-old, Grade II listed building on a street off Rougier Street. The name usually derives from the game of skittles or nine-pins, especially popular in the 18th and 19th centuries. The difficult corner pin was on the outside of the nine skittles set out on a board. The sign here, though, would suggest something a little more civil engineering related. It was the Unicorn until 1985.

THE MALTINGS

Tanner's Moat
Tanner's Moat, York YO1 6HU
01904 655387
www.maltings.co.uk

This excellent pub was originally called the Railway Tavern (because it was near York's two railway stations), and later The Lendal Bridge Inn (because it is just off the bridge); it was established in 1842. The current owner purchased the pub from Bass in 1992, and renamed it The Maltings.

It is next door to what was Botterill's Repository for Horses, built in 1884 and reduced in height by a half in 1965 when it became a car dealer. Patrick Nuttgens described the original building as 'an exotic red and yellow Byzantine building with ramps inside, up which the horses were led to their stalls – a kind of multi-story horse car park'. It was frequently used by patrons of the 1868 Yorkshire Club for gentlemen (River House) in from the country, just over Lendal Bridge.

Lendal Bridge was opened in 1863 to replace the ferry that plied between the Lendal and Barker Towers. Jon Leeman was the last ferryman – he received £15 and a horse and cart in redundancy compensation. The bridge was designed by the aptly named William Dredge. Unfortunately, his bridge collapsed during construction killing five men; it was replaced by the present bridge, designed by Thomas Page who was responsible also for Skeldergate Bridge here and Westminster Bridge. The remnants of Dredge's bridge were dredged up from the river and sold to Scarborough Council who used the remnants in the construction of Valley Bridge.

The gentleman in the foreground is friend of forty years Paul Taylor, poet and trombonist with, among other bands, the Yiddish Twist Orchestra (www.trombonepoetry.com).

YORK TAP

York Railway Station
Station Rd, York YO24 1AB
01904 659009
www.Yorktap.com

'Well worth missing your train for', so says one of the (true for a change) online comments. It is a wonderful conversion from the old York Model Railway. Both rooms are exquisitely furnished and the ambience is excellent. The building, which was built in the early 1900s, features restored original fireplaces and stained-glass windows and skylights.

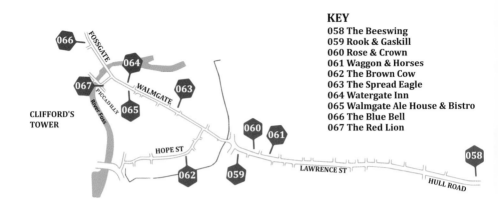

WALMGATE BAR

Originally known as Walbesgate, this is the only York Bar with its barbican still intact, thanks largely to William Etty RA who campaigned tirelessly for its preservation. In 1489 it was set on fire by rebels and later bombarded in the Civil War. The inner facade is 16th century and still retains its Doric and Ionic columns.

Walmgate was a place of great poverty, crime, alcohol-related violence and prostitution, like Hungate, for many years. The infant mortality rate was one in three before age one – as highlighted by Seebohm Rowntree's ground-breaking *Poverty: A Study in Town Life* in 1901 for which researchers visited 11,500 families and found that 25 per cent of the city population was visibly poor – in 'obvious want and squalor'. The pungent smell of hide, skins and fat from local industries added to the horror of the place. At the end of the 1880s there were 8000 midden privies in York, many here and in Hungate. In Walmgate in 1913, the death rate was twenty-three per 1,000, almost twice York's average. Using powers under the 1930 Housing Act, York Corporation began to clear the slums: streets off Walmgate and in Hungate were demolished, and residents moved to new estates outside the city centre.

One of the key industries and employers in Walmgate was The Walker Iron Foundry. Founded in 1837 by John Walker (1801–1853) 'Iron & brass founder, bell-hanger & smith', in Dixon's Yard, Walmgate. They provided the first gas lamps and railings for St Leonard's Place, the gates at Dean's Park and the surrounding railings and gas lights. In 1845–1846 Walker supplied the gates to Kew Gardens, a commission that earned them the patronage of Queen Victoria in 1847 when she granted them permission to describe themselves as 'Ironfounders & Purveyors of Smithy Work to the Queen'. In 1853 they supplied the ten-ton gates and railings to the British Museum, London. Other commissions included gates at Sandringham, the Botanical Gardens in Mauritius and the palace of the Maharajah Holkar of India. Renamed Thomlinson-Walker, the firm moved to the Victoria Foundry at 76 Walmgate.

The Bar from a 19th century watercolour.

THE BEESWING

Hull Road
55 Hull Road, York YO10 3JP
01904 422050

The Beeswing is named after the racehorse (1833–1854) who won the Ascot Gold Cup in 1842 and the Doncaster Gold Cup three times. In her heyday Beeswing – a bay mare out of Dr Syntax – was regarded as the best mare in Britain and one of the greatest of all time. Of her sixty-three races, she won an amazing fifty-one times. Of her fifty-seven finishes she was placed lower than second only once. The town of Lochend in Dumfries and Galloway changed its name to Beeswing in her honour.

An alternative derivation is beeswing as in the delicate crust on a good bottle of port.

Before the success of the bay mare, the pub was simply a Black Swan. Not every sign painter appreciated the provenance of the new name, however: bees started to appear painted into the artwork …

The kitchen here doubled as a bar; family and customers shared the only urinal, which was plagued with bad drainage.

Seen through the Bar.

ROOK & GASKILL

Lawrence Street
12 Lawrence St, York YO10 3WP
01904 655450
www.rookandgaskillYork.co.uk

Messrs Peter Rook and Leonard Gaskill were sheep rustlers from Beverley, who on May 1, 1776, became the last two men to be hanged at the St Leonard's Gallows at Greendykes in York. Their crime was steeling thirteen sheep from John Brown of Driffield.

The pub was previously called the Wheatsheaf, the Princess Victoria in 1834 and then the Queen's Head or the Queen Victoria in 1843. In 1847 it was the Queen Inn. It changed again in 2002 when York Brewery refitted and renamed it to chime with the gallows theme of its first two pubs: The Last Drop Inn and The Three Legged Mare.

ROSE AND CROWN

Lawrence Street
13 Lawrence St, York YO10 3BP
01904 659393
www.roseandcrownYork.com

This was a former Tetley Ale House that had its own brewery. Originally, it was two amalgamated houses from the early 18th century.

WAGGON & HORSES

Lawrence Street
19 Lawrence St, York YO10 3BP
01904 637478
www.waggonandhorsesYork.com

Known as the Waggon and, from 1795,
the Waggon & Horses.

Les Almond takes aim in the bar billiards…

THE BROWN COW

Hope Street
36 Hope Street, York YO10 4UR
01904 634010

This establishment was first recorded in
1834 when it was nameless until 1838.
Other names were the Cow (1843) and the
Dun Cow (1849). Family food was kept in
the cellar; the family shared the WC with
customers. A rebuild opened in 1906. In
1939 the Brown Cow hosted half a darts
match, the other half being played out in the
Ark in Maidenhead – the two teams were
linked by radio.

THE SPREAD EAGLE

Walmgate
98 Walmgate, York YO1 9TL
01904 635868

The Waterside when it was the Five Lions, about 1990 and (below) in the 1950s

WATERGATE INN

Walmgate

24 Walmgate, York YO1 9TJ
01904 625124
www.thewatergateinn.co.uk

The Five Lions until recently, The Watergate Inn is a former coaching inn – the City Arms from 1702 – with a large outside space to the back that goes down to the River Foss. It once had extensive stabling that could cater for fifty horses. The stables have been converted into en-suite guest accommodation and the manure heap has been replaced with a riverside garden. In 1818 the name changed to the Five Lions, continuing the York city arms theme. An early pub sign featured the Latin inscription *vino bono non opus est hedera* – a good wine needs no bush. The gist was that good wines have no need of a bush – the sign of a hostelry – good wine sells itself.

WALMGATE ALE HOUSE & BISTRO
(formerly Meltons Too)

Walmgate
25 Walmgate, York YO1 9TX
01904 629222
www.walmgateale.co.uk

THE BLUE BELL

Fossgate
53 Fossgate, York, YO1 9TF
01904 654904

This, York's smallest pub, and one of the best, was opened in 1798 when the back of the pub faced on to Fossgate and the front was in Lady Peckett's Yard. It was one of two local Blue Bells – the other was in Walmgate. In 1845 it was the meeting place of the Chartist Cooperative Land Society, an ill-conceived organisation that urged working class people to become self-sufficient, spurning factory for field.

Inside the Blue Bell smoke room, now smokeless. Courtesy and © Geoff Brandwood/CAMRA

The Quaker, largely teetotal Rowntrees were responsible for physically turning it around in 1903, no doubt because one of their temperance-preaching adult schools happened to be in Lady Peckett's Yard right behind the pub. It is York's only Grade II* listed Edwardian décor pub with its unaltered 1903 interior. The Blue Bell hosted fundraising meetings to raise the £2,000 needed to buy land for a ground at Fulfordgate (Eastwood Avenue) for the nascent York City and, later, York City FC held their board meetings here; in World War II it served as a soup kitchen. Women were barred from the public bar until as recently as the 1990s. Drinking is encouraged in the narrow corridor where a drop-down seat gives some rest to the weary.

Since 1903, the licence has changed hands only six times. George Robinson, founding director of York City FC, took over that year. When he died in 1948, the licence passed to his wife, Annie. When she passed away in 1963, their daughter Edith Pinder took over, and she remained until retiring in 1991.

THE RED LION

Merchantgate

2 Merchantgate, York YO1 9TU
01904 640418
www.York-pubs.co.uk/theredlion

The Red Lion is built on 13th century foundations, with a 14th–15th century superstructure; a bread oven has been discovered dating from the 14th century; it now resides in the front bar. The pub has two side wings of c.1600. It claims to be the oldest building in York to be used as a pub, though it has only been licensed since 1783, known then as the Three Cups, indicating a connection with the Company of Salters' who would have been active in the fish market that was located here. The pub formerly opened off Fossgate, which with Walmgate, had twenty-eight pubs. It was behind the Black Horse, Fossgate, that served the old pig market on Foss Bridge. The tethering rings for the pigs are still visible on the bridge. The name changed to the Red Lion after 1805 to avoid confusion with another Three Cups on nearby Foss Bridge.

Henry Hunt Heath was landlord in the late 1890s; he also owned the Crown Brewery Hotel in Walmgate.

The pub is notable for its priest hole, hidden between two bedrooms and up one of the chimneys; the Red Lion was presumably a refuge for York recusants when the building was probably a private dwelling. There is a legend that Dick Turpin hid here and escaped through a window.

Priest holes were typically tiny and cramped, with no room to stand up or move around. During a raid the priest would have to stay as still and silent as possible, sometimes for days at a time if necessary. Food and drink would be in very short supply and sanitation non-existent. Sometimes, priests died in a priest hole from starvation or from lack of oxygen. Meanwhile, outside, the priest-hunters or 'pursuivants' would be scrupulously measuring the footprints to and from the house from the outside and the inside to see if they tallied; they would count the windows outside and again from the inside; they would tap on the walls to see if they were hollow and they would rip up floorboards to search underneath. Other priest holes in York are at the Bar Convent and in York Castle, in a part now demolished.

There are around 900 Red Lions in the UK, exceeded only by the 1,000 or so Crowns, many of which will have been crown property at one time or another.

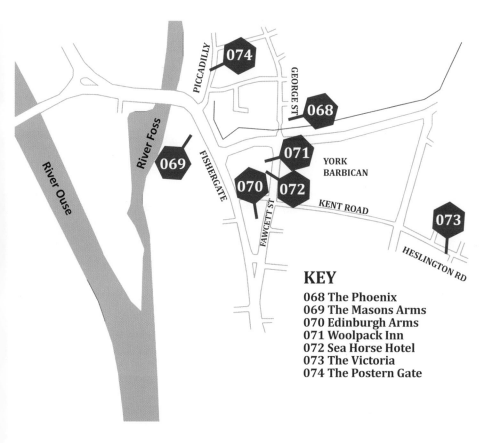

KEY
068 The Phoenix
069 The Masons Arms
070 Edinburgh Arms
071 Woolpack Inn
072 Sea Horse Hotel
073 The Victoria
074 The Postern Gate

FISHERGATE BAR

Sometimes called St George's Bar, this is the gateway to Selby; chains ran across the River Foss here to the castle to reinforce York's defences. In Elizabethan times it was a prison for rascals and lunatics. Fishergate Bar was walled up in 1489 as punishment for the locals who had rioted against a tax levied to pay for a war against Brittany; it was reopened to provide access to the new cattle market in 1827.

THE PHOENIX

George Street
75 George Street, York YO1 9PT
01904 656 401
www.phoenixinnYork.co.uk/
Content/History.html

The original name until the mid-1800s was The Labour in Vain. The sign depicted a white woman vigorously scrubbing a black baby in a frantic bid to make it white; her labours, of course, were in vain. The inscription read 'You may wash him and scrub him from morn till night; your labour's in vain, black will never come white'.

Surprisingly perhaps, there are still a few pubs that have this name: one is in Yarnfield, Stone, in Staffordshire and another in Stourbridge in the West Midlands. Ann Jolly was the landlady here in 1939; her husband, John Jolly, had run a pub on King's Staith, also called the Labour in Vain. When Ann Jolly died, the pub took the name the Black Boy, a reference to the black baby on the sign.

Today's more prosaic name derives from 1876 from the Phoenix Iron Foundry, which stood nearby before it moved in the mid-1870s to a new site on Leeman Road. The pub goes as far back as the late eighteenth century, although what you see inside now comes courtesy of a late 19th-century refit. The Phoenix Inn is the last surviving pub inside the city walls which served the old cattle market, held behind Fishergate Bar until 1827.

THE MASONS ARMS

Fishergate
6 Fishergate, York YO10 4AB
01904 541479
www.masonsarmsYork.co.uk

It was in 1835 that a stonemason, George Tilney, first applied here for a licence to sell alcohol at was called the Quiet Woman. The Quiet Woman sign depicted a woman carrying her decapitated head. Nagging woman meets her fate? It is a common name often accompanied by sexist rhymes along the lines of 'Here is a woman who has lost her head/She's quiet now – you see she's dead'.

Tilney was at first turned down but eventually won his licence and changed the name to the Masons Arms to celebrate his trade. The River Ouse is close by and it was into this river in 1868 that Jane Ketch fell and drowned on leaving the pub, worse for wear on brandy and water.

Rebuilt in 1935 in Tudor style the new Masons Arms was a flagship pub for Tadcaster Tower Brewery. The interior exudes York history, including oak panelling, which comes from nearby York prison; the fireplace was originally in the Castle gatehouse.

EDINBURGH ARMS

Fishergate
25 Fishergate, York, YO10 4AE
01904 623085

This was once called the Edinboro Castle and the Edinburgh Arms.

WOOLPACK INN

Fawcett Street
6 Fawcett St, York YO10 4AH
01904 611060
www.woolpackinnYork.com

SEA HORSE HOTEL

Fawcett Street
4 Fawcett Street, York, YO10 4AH
01904 624574

THE VICTORIA

Heslington Road
1 Heslington Road, York YO10 5AR
01904 622295
www.victoriahotelYork.co.uk

An Old Mill Brewery pub, established in 1983, Old Mill Brewery is a small independent family owned brewery, housed in an 18th century former corn mill and maltings at Snaith in East Yorkshire.

THE POSTERN GATE

Piccadilly
90 Piccadilly, York YO1 9NX
01904 526220

This pub was named after the three-storey Fishergate Postern (previously the Talkan Tower) – *posternam iuxta Skarletpit* – and dates from 1502. It is York's only surviving example. Buildings adjoining the postern were destroyed in a 1489 riot. The tower was originally called Edward's Tower. A projecting lavatory discharged into the adjacent King's Pool. Dick Turpin's grave is nearby in the garden on the site of St George's church. He was executed on 7 April 1739 after spending time in a cell, which can still be seen in the Debtor's Prison in the Castle Museum.

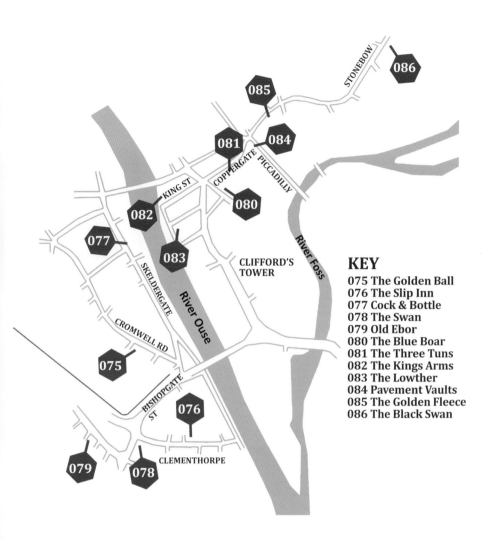

KEY

075 The Golden Ball
076 The Slip Inn
077 Cock & Bottle
078 The Swan
079 Old Ebor
080 The Blue Boar
081 The Three Tuns
082 The Kings Arms
083 The Lowther
084 Pavement Vaults
085 The Golden Fleece
086 The Black Swan

OTHER YORK PUBS

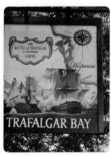

THE GOLDEN BALL

Cromwell Road
2 Cromwell Rd, Bishophill, York YO1 6DU
01904 849040
www.goldenballYork.co.uk

The Golden Ball dates back to the late 18th century with its first mention in newspapers of 1773. Charles Dickens may well have drunk here: Mr Micawber from *David Copperfield*, is based on a Richard Chicken, a feckless character who in 1847 worked in the same York railway office as Albert Dickens, Charles' railway engineer brother. Chicken, who lived opposite the pub, was also an actor and at one time a self-styled Professor of Elocution and Lecturer on Defective Annunciation.

The pub was increased in size in 1883 when the old 'Jail Lane' was widened to make what is now Cromwell Road. The jail, and gallows, used to be at the bottom of the street at Baile Hill. John Smith's bought the pub in 1902 and in 1929 their refurbishment included the unique bar-side seating alcove. This from *The English Heritage Advice Report*:

> The Golden Ball is designated Grade II as a largely complete example of an inter-war scheme in a small urban pub … The unusual plan-form dating back to the 1929 refurbishment incorporates the only known example of a bar side seating alcove (the snug). There is a high level of survival of fixtures and fittings relating to the 1920s scheme, including doors, architraves, terrazzo flooring, back-fitting, hinged counters and sashed screen-work to both ends of the servery, fire surround to the public bar, glazed cream and geometric patterned tilework to public bar counter front and dado level in entrance lobby and out-sales (jug and bottle). The use of glazed tilework externally in the brown glazed brickwork and permanent signage on tiled fascia and internally in the entrance lobby, public bar, and out-sales is both cohesive to the design and representative of the inter-war period.

There was also a clubroom for the playing of brass instruments.

The website says it all:

> Welcome to The Golden Ball, York's first community co-operative pub in the heart of Bishophill. We are a Grade II listed pub with a well preserved Victorian layout and lovely tiled bar … We also sell fresh, local free range eggs from Johnson's in Terrington, who deliver direct to the pub each week, and amazing artisan bread hand made by Al from BlueBird Bakery, just around the corner. The bread is delivered most teatimes, so call in for a loaf and a pint!
>
> Our focus is on the community and we have a range of events and community groups using the pub. We have hosted weddings, christenings,

weekly baby groups, choirs, children's Christmas parties and Pensioners History talks, gardening events and coffee mornings, clothes swaps and charity fundraisers. We have regular craft fairs and art exhibitions too.

A true community pub and only one of twelve in the country at the time.

THE SLIP INN

Clementhorpe
20 Clementhorpe, York YO23 1AN
01904 621793

The Ouse Navigation Trustees built the slipway at Clementhorpe in 1836, which gives its name to the pub there. Terry's moved to their purpose-built Baroque Revival building in 1930 from the Clementhorpe site, which they had occupied since 1862. By 1840 Terry's products were being delivered to seventy-five towns all over England; products included candied eringo, coltfoot rock, gum balls and lozenges made from squill, camphor and horehound. Apart from boiled sweets, they also made marmalade, marzipan, mushroom ketchup and calves' jelly. Conversation lozenges, precursors of Love Hearts (with such slogans as 'Can you polka?', 'I want a wife', 'Do you love me?' and 'How do you flirt?'), were particularly popular. Chocolate production began around 1867 on Clementhorpe with thirteen chocolate products adding to the other 380 or so confectionery and parfait lines. Before World War II 'Theatre Chocolates' were available with rustle-proof wrappers. The famous Chocolate Orange (which started life as a Chocolate Apple) was born in 1932 and at one point one in ten Christmas stockings reputedly contained a Terry's Chocolate Orange. In the 1990s seven million boxes of All Gold were sold in a year.

COCK & BOTTLE

Skeldergate
61 Skeldergate, York YO1 6DS
01904 654165

The name is believed to refer to the availability of liquor in draught or bottles, 'cock' being the name for the tap in the front of a barrel. Cock & Bottle clearly indicates that beer is available by the bottle and by the barrel. Former names are The Plumber's Arms and Duke's Place. The building we see today is a rebuild of the original – demolished to widen Skeldergate.

THE SWAN

Bishopgate Street
16 Bishopgate Street, York YO23 1JH
01904 634968
www.theswanyork.co.uk

The Swan is a small, two-roomed, traditional ale-house on the corner of Clementhorpe, blessed with a beautifully preserved Grade II-listed 'nationally important' 1930s interior and a warm and inclusive ambience. Dating from about 1857, this Swan started life as a grocery shop, with a sideline in beers: owner Thomas Staverly got the name from seven cygnets he saw on the Ouse, which had been purchased by York Corporation. By 1897 it was a beerhouse right and proper. In 1936 Tetley's knocked it down and rebuilt it.

OLD EBOR

Drake Street
2 Drake St, York YO23 1EQ
01904 629954

Another York pub hugging the city walls, it was built in the latter half of the 19th century with the Old in its name added to distinguish it from other inns of the time called Ebor. Ebor is, of course, short for Eboracum, York, as founded in 71 CE by Roman governor Petilius Cerialis and named Eboracum by geographer Ptolemy. Eboracum is derived from the Common Brittonic Eburākon, which means 'yew tree place'.

Ebor Day is part of the four-day Yorkshire Ebor Festival traditionally held at the Knavesmire in mid-August also featuring Ladies' Day. The Ebor is the oldest (it dates from the 1840) and most famous York race, and the richest handicap in Europe.

THE BLUE BOAR

Castlegate
5 Castlegate, York YO1 9RN
01904 593209

Before reverting to the Blue Boar, this pub was called the Little John; the original Blue Boar closed in 1775 but some historians argue that the Little John and the Blue Boar were entirely different and that the Little John was previously known as the Robin Hood from the 1700s, changing its name to Little John in 1893. At that time, a sign was placed in the pub, reading: 'Robin Hood is dead and gone, now come and drink with Little John.'

The Blue Boar is a traditional British alehouse dating back to the early 1700s. Coaches to Selby ran from there three days a week under the name Providence, and later Diligence.

Highwayman Dick Turpin, also known as John Palmer, ended his days there: he was hanged (somewhat fittingly) on the Knavesmire in 1739, for horse stealing – 'a crime worthy of death'. Turpin had spent his last six months in the Debtors' Prison where he had many visitors: his jailer is said to have earned £100 from selling drinks to Turpin and his guests; Turpin bought a new frock coat and shoes and hired five mourners for £3.10s for the occasion. A report in *The Gentleman's Magazine* for 7 April 1739 notes Turpin's arrogance: 'Turpin behaved in an undaunted manner; as he mounted the ladder, feeling his right leg tremble, he spoke a few words to the topsman, then threw himself off, and expir'd in five minutes.' The short drop method of hanging meant that those executed were killed by slow strangulation: Turpin was left swinging until late afternoon, before being cut down and taken to The Blue Boar Inn in Castlegate and laid out in the cellar.

Turpin's grave in St George's churchyard was dug particularly deep to confound body snatchers; to no avail: the corpse was removed and found later at the back of Stonegate in a surgeon's garden. Before reburial, the coffin was filled with lime.

In 1828 William Maude took on the licence; he was the former owner of the Commercial Coffee House on Ousegate.

THE THREE TUNS

Coppergate
12 Coppergate, York YO1 9NR
01904 673097

The Three Tuns was established in 1782. There are plenty of low beams and architectural character to be had in this; it is one of York's oldest pubs. However, in 1832 it was known as the Yorkshireman Coffee House, then just the Yorkshireman. In 1898 Thackeray's Brewery established their head office in the pub. Renovation work in the next century revealed a stash of gold coin, some pieces dating back to Charles I. The Three Tuns name came in 1930; the sign is based on the Vintner's Coat of Arms, which is a sable and chevron enarched between three tuns.

Beer casks come in the following sizes: firkin: 9 gallons; kilderkin: 18 gallons; barrel: 36 gallons; hogshead: 54 gallons; tun: 216 gallons.

THE KINGS ARMS

King's Staith
3 King's Staith, York YO1 9SN
01904 659435

This is an early 17th century building on King's Staith, traditionally a hotbed of crime and prostitution. Originally, the pub had no fireplaces or room partitions so it may have been a custom house, or a warehouse. Very thick walls protect it from floods, which recur to this day with alarming regularity. Due to the flooding, the cellars are on the first floor. Bodies of criminals were laid out here before being hung on and then flung from old Ouse Bridge just along the staith.

It was first recorded as a pub in 1783 or 1795 as the Kings Arms; then in the 19th century licensee George Duckitt renamed it as Ouse Bridge Inn. It reverted to its old name in 1974. The inn sign depicts King Richard III, who as a boy grew up at Middleham Castle, and as Duke of Gloucester visited York frequently from his castle at Sheriff Hutton. He was very popular in York.

The Kings Arms is 'the pub that floods'; it is the pub that is never dry. On the right hand side of the door is a board with the flood levels marked on it. In 2000 the water was six feet deep in the bar, deep enough to drown your sorrows in. Every time York floods – and that's a lot of times – the pub provides the backdrop for news reports the world over.

The devastating floods of Christmas 2014.

King's Staith in 1845 with the King's Arms, the white building to the left of centre.

THE LOWTHER

Cumberland Street
8 Cumberland Street, York, YO1 9SW
01904) 622987
www.thelowther.co.uk

Just as prone to flooding is the Lowther next door. And like the Kings Arms it's on the banks of the Ouse. The ground floor is raised several feet above the staith to minimise flooding.

The Lowther shipping floodwater in 2014.   The Lowther on a sunnier day in 2015.

PAVEMENT VAULTS

Pavement
2 Piccadilly, York YO1 9NU
01904 670777
www.pavementvaults.co.uk

Pavement Vaults (1942) and its earlier incarnations are steeped in history. It was trading as the Board in the 1880s when brewers J.J. Hunt bought the premises and business of William Cooper, wine and spirit merchant. The 'unsightly old property' was replaced in 1893 with a new jettied and pargeted building, resplendent with a Burmantoft ware entrance hall.

Pavement Vaults on Pavement, 1965 with wine store to the left and Golden Fleece to the right.

Originally, it was on Pavement, a medieval street dating back to 1378, but was wrecked in order to make way for Piccadilly.

Prior to the demolition the site was a coaching inn. The White Swan Hotel was built on the site 1912 and the 'Centre Bar', housed within the hotel, was 'a popular hangout for York's young hedonists', whatever they were. The hotel finally closed in 1982.

For the full story of the Vaults, go to http://Yorkstories.co.uk/buildings/white-swan-hotel-piccadilly/.

Pavement was a veritable menagerie and a hive of activity; all life was here. *Ye Old Streete of Pavement,* written by W. Camidge in 1893 and published by the *Yorkshire Gazette* provides a colourful, vivid picture of activity there over the years. We read of the Goose Flags – the path in front of St Crux signifying the goose market there; boots and shoes on sale 'in Whip-ma-whop-ma-gate, where members of the "Worshipful Company of Translators" sold these commodities, old and new' and 'the basket market … at the bottom of Colliergate'. The pleasure fairs 'at Whitsuntide and Martinmas', and the shows that accompanied them, were very popular too: there were dog and lion fights 'and other shows with fat women, deformed men, giants and dwarfs, reptiles, waxworks, mechanical inventions, fortune tellers, circuses, boxing booths' along with swing boats and hobby horses. Peep shows were particularly popular.

> their incidents stirring, and their pictures very striking … chiefly battles … Waterloo and the crossing of the Alps by Napoleon … described by the showman in measured and monotonous tones in which fact and fancy were mixed up in most bewildering confusion.

THE GOLDEN FLEECE

Pavement
23 Peasholme Green, York YO1 7PR
01904 679131

The ancient Golden Fleece still survives with its impressive golden sheep hanging above the door. The pub is reputedly haunted, home to no fewer than seven ghosts. Earliest mention of the building is in the City Archive of 1503; it originally belonged to The Merchant Adventurers who named it to celebrate and maintain their thriving trade in wool. In 1666 we get our first reference to it as a pub. In 1702, John Peckett, Lord Mayor, owned it. In 1733 it was known as the Fleece Inn. The building has dodgy foundations which accounts in part for its lop-sidedness. The sheep sign was blown down in 1900 or so causing the sheep to lose its legs and its head.

It is York's second oldest continuously licensed premises – dating back to 1668. The frontage is mid-19th century, but rear parts go back to 16th century, and are what is left of a courtyard for coaches: the Golden Fleece was a major coaching inn in the 18th and early 19th centuries.

The jetty of Thomas Herbert's House (the largest surviving town house in the UK) and Lady Peckett's Yard projects into a side passage, once the only way in to the pub. In 1667, Richard Booth, a York merchant, was allowed to mint his own copper halfpennies which are shown as produced 'at the Golden Fleece'.

As noted above in the description of the White Swan in Goodramgate, when both the Golden Fleece and the White Swan each applied for a licence to install a newfangled juke box, York's Chief Constable refused, describing them as 'unsuitable and undesirable instruments to have in a public house bar or lounge'. Drinking yourself stupid was fine though.

Long-standing customer sitting at the bar.   Bored to death?

THE BLACK SWAN

Peasholme Green

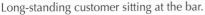

A fine former mid-16th century merchant's mansion, the Black Swan is in Peasholme Green and is another former coaching station. Seriously haunted and also known as The Mucky Duck, it is one of the oldest licensed houses in York. Originally, though, it was the home of William Bowes, former Sheriff, Mayor and MP between 1417 and 1428. His great grandson was Sir Martyn Bowes. He eventually became Lord Mayor of London and goldsmith to Elizabeth I. Bowes had a great love for York and gave to the City a Sword of State, which is still used on ceremonial occasions.

The upstairs room was the venue for illegal cockfights; the grill used by the guard to watch the stairs can still be seen. In 1710 the pub hosted a social gathering of the Innholders Company after their court meeting in St Anthony's Hall opposite. It is

Off for a day out from the Black Swan in 1905.   first recorded as a pub, the Swan, in

1787. In 1808 Mrs Weston hit the headlines when she gave birth to a baby boy in the pub. Mrs Weston proudly showed her son around the city in the light of the press interest: 'extraordinary diminutive of the human species, though without deformity, being but 34 inches high'.

The pub still has a fine oak staircase and a magnificent Delft fireplace. The staircase leads upstairs to the 'Trompe D'Oeil' room. This means 'deceiving the eye'; the room is so called because the woodwork is painted to look like elaborate panelling. In World War II the pub was utilised as a horse refuge, a reflection of the ample stabling available there.

General Wolfe's family lived here; it was the HQ of the York Layerthorpe Cycling Club from 1834. The Leeds Arms (closed 1935) was next door on the corner of Haymarket; the Woolpack was over the road.

The house later passed to the Thompson family, who also owned the Olde Starre Inne on Stonegate. Henry Thompson, who was Sheriff in 1601, was a Wine Merchant. Edward Thompson, born in 1670, had a country seat at the Old Hall, Long Marston, and used this house on Peasholme Green as his town house. His daughter Henrietta Thompson married Colonel Edward Wolfe in 1724 at Long Marston. Thereafter, the couple resided at the house here on Peasholme Green, but in July 1726 moved to Westerham, Kent, where James Wolfe was born on 2 January 1727. As General Wolfe, he died taking Quebec from the French, and so laid the foundations of British Canada.

The White Swan in the early 1900s, with Leeds Arms to the right.

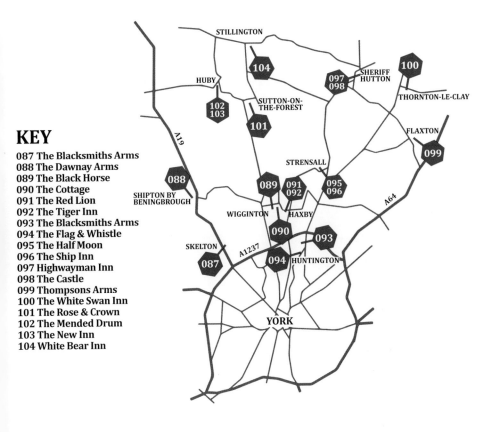

KEY

087 The Blacksmiths Arms
088 The Dawnay Arms
089 The Black Horse
090 The Cottage
091 The Red Lion
092 The Tiger Inn
093 The Blacksmiths Arms
094 The Flag & Whistle
095 The Half Moon
096 The Ship Inn
097 Highwayman Inn
098 The Castle
099 Thompsons Arms
100 The White Swan Inn
101 The Rose & Crown
102 The Mended Drum
103 The New Inn
104 White Bear Inn

IN THE VILLAGES: NORTH

THE BLACKSMITHS ARMS

Skelton
Shipton Road, Skelton, York YO30 1XW
01904 471902

THE DAWNAY ARMS

Shipton
Main St, Shipton by Beningbrough, York YO30 1AB
01904 470334
www.thedawnayarms.co.uk

Shipton is not really 'by' Beningborough at all – the villages are nearly two miles apart. The connection exists because Shipton formed part of the Beningbrough Estate, which was owned first by the Bourdner and then the Dawnay families. Independence came in 1917 when the estate was dissolved. In 1655, Ann Middleton bequeathed £1,000 to a grammar school in the village and twenty shillings a year to feed the local poor. The school was demolished in 1850 when Payan Dawnay built a new one. The public house named after the family was originally The Bay Horse, built in 1730. The splendid family Coat of Arms graces the door and the pub sign.

The Black Horse in the early 20th century. Originally published in Hugh Murray's *A Directory of York Pubs*.

THE BLACK HORSE

Wigginton
42–44 The Village, Wigginton, York YO32 2PJ
01904 758473

The Black Horse was first mentioned in 1840.

For a list of all hostelries called the Black Horse, visit www.black-horse-pub.com. This site is the eccentric creation of Joe Bratton who tells us:

it's better than stamp collecting ... This website is about the history of the inn sign Black Horse, the theory is that it may be connected to Arthurian legend in that Black Horse pubs may be in places of Romano Brit[ish] victories against the invading Saxons. It lists every Black Horse pub, inn or hotel in the UK and the World and includes the numerous Black Horse pubs that have closed down, been demolished or have scandalously changed names. but mainly ... it catalogues one man's quest to visit every Black Horse pub and, hopefully, enjoy one of their pints.

In all, there are apparently 330 such named places – beaten by the 350 White Horses. See the Bay Horse, Blossom Street, for his theory on the origin of this name.

THE COTTAGE

Haxby
115 The Village, Haxby, York YO32 2JH
01904 763949
www.thecottageinnhaxby.com/index

Formerly a private residence called Beet Cottage, now it is The Cottage pub which opened in September 1980. Here are some bar prices from 1980:

Stout – 31p
Bitter – 45p (bar), 47p (lounge)
Lager – 52p (bar), 54p (lounge)
Vodka – 42p
Babycham – 41p

THE RED LION

Haxby
52 The Village, Haxby, York YO32 2HX
01904 760761

The Red Lion appears on Ordnance Survey maps from the mid-19th century. Apart from its function as a hostelry the Red Lion also served as an 18th-century business centre: the meeting to finalise the construction of the two miles of the Foss Navigation north of Haxby was held here in May 1795 with a cost of £460 being agreed with contactors John Harrison & Co.

The Red Lion, Haxby in 1906. Originally published in Hugh Murray's *A Directory of York Pubs*.

THE TIGER INN

Haxby
29 The Village, North Yorkshire, York, York YO32 3HS
01904 768355

Another old Haxby village tavern is the Tiger Inn, first mentioned in records in 1840 when two cottages and a blacksmith's were converted to make it into a public house.

BLACKSMITH'S ARMS

Huntington
56 The Old Village, Huntington
York YO32 9RB
01904 752940
www.blacksmithsarms-huntington.co.uk

The pub dates from 1823. It was known as the Hammer & Pincers from 1872–1876.

An RAF Wellington bomber crashed on the houses opposite the Blacksmith's Arms on the afternoon of 14 April 1943. The MK10 Wellington was from 429 Squadron, Royal Air Force based at Eastmoor and on a training flight when an engine fire caused it to crash. The pilot and four other crew were killed along with three ladies on the ground; the cottages were rebuilt with one of them appropriately named 'Phoenix'.

THE FLAG and WHISTLE

Huntington
Huntington Road, Huntington YO32 9PX
01904 769200

The old York–Hull line ran through New Earswick and stopped at Earswick railway station until its closure in 1965. The aptly named The Flag and Whistle pub now stands on the site, built in 1982. The pub was built to serve the village of New Earswick, but it is actually in the parish of Huntington due to a covenant placed on New Earswick, which keeps it a dry village of Quaker origins established by Joseph Rowntree. The objective of the Joseph Rowntree Trust when it developed the idea of the new garden village was to provide the worker with even the lowest means a new type of house that was clean, sanitary and efficient. Rowntree's deep concern for the welfare of his workers, the research findings of his son, Seebohm, into the plight of the urban poor, his Quaker beliefs and the pioneering work on garden cities by Ebenezer Howard all combined to drive Rowntree's New Earswick.

THE HALF MOON

Strensall
3 The Village, Strensall, York, YO32 5XS
01904 492919
www.halfmoonstrensall.co.uk

Henry Nattriss was the landlord in 1890. The pub's name may reflect the old tradition where large houses (including those owned by the Church as here) were often open to travellers for food and drink; signs such as a half moon would have indicated that, as in this case, the (public) house was a place of refreshment. Alternatively, it may be connected with the Earl of Northumberland whose badge was a half moon; the Earl was a friend of William Poteman, Prebendary of Strensall. The existing building was rebuilt in 1830 on the site of the earlier tavern. Messers Bellerby and Jackson owned the pub in 1849. The building projecting out into the street on the left was Bellerby Square, now demolished.

THE SHIP INN

Strensall
23 The Village, Strensall, York YO32 5XS
01904 490302
www.theshipinn-strensall.co.uk

Why a pub called The Ship so many miles from the sea? The Ship was a popular watering hole for travellers on the Foss Navigation and workers at the tannery behind from the early 1900s. Opened in 1806 as Hirst & Sons, the tannery was able to benefit from the Foss Navigation that had opened as far as Strensall in 1797, with the extension to Sheriff Hutton Bridge begun in 1801. The Navigation passed conveniently nearby for the delivery of materials such as bark and lime and the despatch of finished goods. *Baines Directory 1890* lists three boot and shoemakers (including another Creaser) and a tanner, William Walker, at the tannery ('oak bark tanners of shaved and dressed hides'). Later owned by Leeds tanners Charles F. Stead & Co., it employed fifty or so people in the 1960s. By the time it closed in 2004 only nine workers remained; since then it has remained derelict and half-demolished until the new Tannery development in 2015.

HIGHWAYMAN INN

Sheriff Hutton
The Square, Sheriff Hutton, York YO60 6QZ
01347 878328
www.thehighwayman.uk.com

THE CASTLE

Sheriff Hutton
Main St, Sheriff Hutton, York, YO60 6ST
01347 878335

Everyone knows that Sheriff Hutton has a castle – what is less well known is that it has, in fact, had two castles. The earlier castle was a Norman motte-and-bailey structure from 1140, of which only the mounds survive. It was built by Ansketil de Bulmer on land given to him by William the Conqueror for his support in the conquest. The Sheriff part of the village's name derives from its connections with the Bulmer family. Ansketil and Bertram de Bulmer were High Sheriffs of Yorkshire in the periods 1115–1128 and 1128–1130, respectively.

THE WHITE SWAN INN

Thornton-le-Clay
Low St, Thornton-le-Clay YO60 7TG
01653 618286
tlcwhiteswan.com

THE ROSE and CROWN

Sutton on the Forest
Main St, Sutton-on-the-Forest, YO61 1DP
01347 811111

Sutton appears in the *Domesday Book* with the following credentials: value to Lord Morcar in 1066 £32; value to lord (King William) in 1086 £1. Twelve villagers, four smallholders and one priest; 27 plough hands, 5.5 men's plough teams; pasture 1.5 leagues; woodland 1 league; 1 mill, value 1.0; 1 church. Before it was a pub the Rose and Crown was a house and a stable.

Sutton had another pub until recently. The Blackwell Ox was originally a private residence built around 1823 for a Mary Shepherd. The name of the pub derives from a shorthorn Teeswater ox registered under the name of The Blackwell Ox, which was bred and raised by Christopher Hill. The ox was six feet tall and weighed 2,278 lb; when it was slaughtered and butchered in 1779 the meat fetched £109 11s 6d.

A fine example of early Georgian architecture, Sutton Park was built by Thomas Atkinson. Apart from his own impressive house at 20 St Saviourgate, York, Atkinson was responsible for remodelling the facade and gatehouse of Bishopthorpe Palace in the 1760s and for the chapel and facade of the Bar Convent in York. Sutton Park is noted for its Rococo plasterwork by Cortese, its collection of 18th-century furniture and its paintings, many of which came from Buckingham Palace.

The Ox in 2011 and in the early 1900s.

THE MENDED DRUM

Huby
Tollerton Rd, Huby, York YO61 1HT
01347 810264
www.themendeddrum.com

In 2009 the pub known as the Star was derelict, with no future. It was in 2011 that a drastic refurbishment started that transformed the old Star into a virtually new pub with a fascinating name. Suggestions for the name were sought from the locals: the new owners' only stipulation was they wanted something with a literary connection in line with their sister pub in York, The Artful Dodger.

The Maypole was a popular suggestion inspired by the village maypole that was erected in front of the pub; the Maypole, however, failed the literary test. In the end, the name that was finally chosen was The Mended Drum. This derives from the Terry Pratchett *Discworld* novels. The pub website fills in the detail:

> [it] seemed very apt for the transformation of the building as in the series; the pub once called The Broken Drum was an establishment with a poor reputation. In the Discworld novel, The Colour of Magic, it was burned to the ground, and when it was rebuilt under new management, it was renamed The Mended Drum. A similar, if not quite exact storyline for The Star.

Permission was sought and granted by Terry Pratchett himself whose next novel was, coincidentally, a version of Charles Dickens', *Oliver Twist*, which he called *Dodger*.

THE NEW INN

Huby
Main St, Huby YO61 1HQ
01347 810393
www.newinnhuby.co.uk

WHITE BEAR INN

Stillington
Main St, Stillington, York YO61 1JU
01347 810338
www.thewhitebearinn-York.co.uk

Thomas Gill would have us believe, in his 1853 history *Vallis Eboracensis*, that the name Stillington derives from Stealing Town – a reputation won by the locals' habit of 'robbing the king's forest of its deer, and the packmen of their merchandise'. Be that as it may, the true derivation of the name is pre-Conquest: *Domesday* has it as 'Stivelincton', held by the Archbishop of York and worth ten shillings a year. Stivel is a Saxon personal name.

Laurence Sterne (1713–1768) was vicar here from 1743. He is reputed to have flung the manuscript of his *The Life and Opinions of Tristram Shandy, Gentleman* onto the fire, when he detected a notable lack of interest amongst his audience at an early reading. It was salvaged and went on to be regarded as one of the greatest comic novels in English. Coxwold is where Sterne is now buried: the first attempt at interment was unsuccessful; his body was exhumed from its Hanover Square in London grave by 'resurrection men' and sold to the Department of Anatomy at Cambridge University. Unfortunately – or fortunately – the Professor of Anatomy, an old friend of Sterne's, recognised the cadaver. Sterne's remains were finally transferred to Coxwold by the Laurence Sterne Trust in 1969.

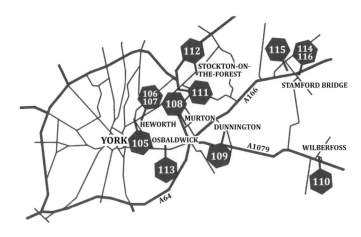

KEY

105 The Shoulder of Mutton
106 The Nag's Head
107 The Walnut Tree
108 Murton Arms
109 The Cross Keys
110 The Oddfellows Arms
111 The Hop Grape
112 The Fox
113 The Derwent Arms
114 The New Inn
115 The Three Cups
116 The Bay Horse

IN THE VILLAGES: EAST

THE SHOULDER OF MUTTON

Heworth
64 Heworth Green, Heworth. York YO31 7TQ
01904 424793
www.theshoulderofmuttonyork.co.uk

The building dates back to 1889 and was a doctors' surgery before it was a pub. It was then renovated into a small hotel. Actor Paul Newman allegedly stayed here at the peak of his career along with other well known celebrities over the years. The pub made the news in 2008 when Mr Watson, the landlord, was ordered to pay £20,000 and knock down a gazebo he had put up for smokers in his beer garden after City of York Council said the use of seven screws in the structure breached planning rules. The words 'screw' and 'loose' spring to mind …

THE NAG'S HEAD

Heworth
56 Heworth Rd, York YO31 0AD
01904 424200
www.nagsheadyork.com

THE WALNUT TREE

Heworth
The Village, Heworth, York YO31 1AN
01904 438922
www.walnuttreeheworth.co.uk

MURTON ARMS
(formerly The Bay Horse)

Murton
Murton Way, Murton, York YO19 5UQ
01904 272262
www.murtonarms.co.uk

The Yorkshire Museum of Farming is at Murton Park; also there is a small railway track, part of the Derwent Valley Light Railway, and York Livestock Centre.

THE CROSS KEYS

Dunnington
3 Common Rd, Dunnington, York YO19 5NG
01904 488847
www.thecrosskeysyork.co.uk

THE ODDFELLOWS ARMS

Wilberfoss
11 Main St, Wilberfoss, York YO41 5NN
01759 388473

The first recorded alehouse here was licensed in 1729, later accompanied by up to four others in houses later in the century. In 1823 there were the Horseshoes or the Blacksmith's Arms (demolished to make way for the bypass), the True Briton, and the Waggon & Horses. The True Briton became the Oddfellows Arms around 1840 and The Waggon & Horses closed before 1872.

There is nothing odd in the name. Odd Fellows (or Oddfellows, Odd Fellowship or Oddfellowship), is an international fraternity consisting of lodges first documented in 1730 in London, the first known lodge being Loyal Aristarcus Lodge No. 9. Convivial meetings were held 'in much revelry and, often as not, the calling of the Watch to restore order'. The names of several pubs today would indicate past Odd Fellows affiliations. The name 'odd fellows' may come from people who practised 'odd trades', who joined together to form a larger group of 'odd fellows'. Even today, Odd Fellows espouse philanthropy, reciprocity, mutual assistance and charity.

THE HOP GROVE

Nr. Stockton-on-the-Forest
Malton Rd, York YO32 9TE
01904 424542

The Hop Grove on Malton Road has been around since 1857 at least. Records refer to it under the name The Hop Pole Inn in 1889 and 1893. This was replaced in the 1930s by the present building. For a short period from 1997 it was renamed The Stockton-on-the-Forest after the nearby village.

THE FOX

Stockton-on-the Forest
90 The Village, Stockton-on-Forest, York YO32 9UW
01904 400747
www.thefoxinnyork.co.uk

THE DERWENT ARMS

Osbaldwick
39 The Village, Osbaldwick, York YO10 3NP
01904 413498
www.thederwentarms.co.uk

114 THE NEW INN

Stamford Bridge
12–14 The Square, Stamford Bridge, York YO41 1AF
01759 371307

Formerly the much more dramatically named **The Swordsman** with its superb sign; the Swordsman was named after the fighting in the crucial battle here in 1066 before the even more crucial battle at Hastings. The New Inn name is devoid of all history.

In the early autumn of 1066, Harold Godwinson's English throne was under serious military threat on two fronts: from Harald Hardrada (with Harold's disaffected and exiled brother, Tostig Godwinson) in the north and from William of Normandy in the south. York capitulated to the Vikings and left Harold in a quandary: to meet Hardrada in battle and then go on to deal with William, or to head south immediately. In the event, Harold came north and joined battle with Harald here at Stamford Bridge winning a total and militarily impressive victory.

The aftermath of the battle is interesting: both Harald and Tostig died in the slaughter; the *Anglo-Saxon Chronicle* tells us that only twenty-four ships were needed to get the Viking survivors home – they had come to Yorkshire in 300. One of its more famous episodes, perhaps a legend, tells us that a Viking warrior, a beserker, stubbornly blocked a bridge over the Derwent, preventing Harold's armies from crossing until a Saxon soldier leaped into the river and stabbed him from beneath. It is featured in the *Anglo-Saxon Chronicle Manuscript C*, but only as a later interpolation.

THE THREE CUPS

Stamford Bridge
York Road, Stamford Bridge, York YO41 1AX
01759 377381
www.vintageinn.co.uk

Stamford Bridge has never been short of public houses. The Three Tuns, recorded in 1823, is lost to us but The Bay Horse and The New Inn, mentioned in records in 1823 and 1840 respectively, remain open. The New Inn, as noted, was renamed The Swordsman in 1974 to celebrate the town's proud Viking heritage. The Jolly Sailors, mentioned in 1840, was possibly The Hope & Anchor, known from 1851 and last recorded in 1892. The Three Cups on York Road is reputedly on the site of a camp for soldiers waiting to take part in the famous battle; an ancient, 23-foot-deep draw well, discovered during building works in the 1960s, can still be seen today through a porthole in the floor.

THE BAY HORSE

Stamford Bridge
4 Church Rd, Stamford Bridge, York YO41 1AA
01759 373028

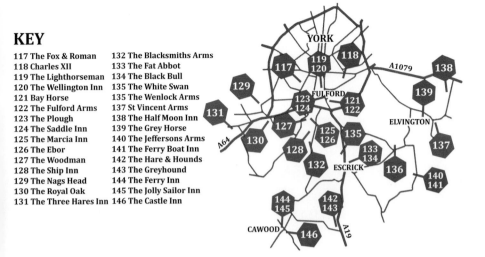

KEY

117 The Fox & Roman
118 Charles XII
119 The Lighthorseman
120 The Wellington Inn
121 Bay Horse
122 The Fulford Arms
123 The Plough
124 The Saddle Inn
125 The Marcia Inn
126 The Ebor
127 The Woodman
128 The Ship Inn
129 The Nags Head
130 The Royal Oak
131 The Three Hares Inn

132 The Blacksmiths Arms
133 The Fat Abbot
134 The Black Bull
135 The White Swan
135 The Wenlock Arms
137 St Vincent Arms
138 The Half Moon Inn
139 The Grey Horse
140 The Jeffersons Arms
141 The Ferry Boat Inn
142 The Hare & Hounds
143 The Greyhound
144 The Ferry Inn
145 The Jolly Sailor Inn
146 The Castle Inn

IN THE VILLAGES: SOUTH

THE FOX & ROMAN

Dringhouses
58 Tadcaster Road, Dringhouses, York YO24 1LR
01904 708720
www.vintageinn.co.uk/thefoxandromanYork

This has an interesting name that both remembers the building's former incarnation as The Fox Hotel from 1822 and refers to a Roman grave found on the site in 1833; some artefacts are on display. The Fox Hotel, opposite York racecourse's stables, used to stable racehorses for the races at the nearby Knavesmire. It was rebuilt in 1900 and tastefully refurbished and extended in 1997; it has retained many original features.

CHARLES XII

Heslington
Main Street, Heslington, York YO10 5EA
01904 426661

There were three alehouses here in the 18th century: in 1823 there was the Robin Hood and The Ship, by 1840 renamed The Bay Horse and The Fox respectively. The Bay Horse was also called the Horse and the Chestnut Horse. It was then rebadged the Charles XII by Voltaire out of Wagtail from the winner of the 1839 St Leger flat race after a rerun after a dead heat. In 1872 The Fox was later called The Yarburgh Arms and renamed again in 1967 as The Deramore Arms.

Lord Deramore was the Lord of the Manor during the 1930s and the owner of Heslington Hall, later to become part of the University of York in the 1960s. Heslington Hall was built in 1568 for Sir Thomas Eynns, who was secretary to the Council of the North from 1550–1578. During World War II it was requisitioned as Headquarters of 64 Group, Bomber Command.

THE LIGHTHORSEMAN

Fulford
124 Fulford Road, York YO10 4BE
01904 624818
www.lighthorseman.co.uk

This is the only pub in the world with this name. This grand Grade II-listed pub has a history dating back to the 1870s; it was built by York architect Walter Green Penty (1852–1902) soon after the Crimean War from where it gets its unique name: specifically the doomed charge of the Light Brigade. A previous pub with the same name on that site appears on the 1852 Ordnance Survey map of York.

The pub enjoys an enduring relationship with the nearby Imphal barracks, which originally accommodated cavalry regiments. The pub may have been used as an officers' mess at one time.

Penty designed Botterill's Horse Repository in Tanner's Moat around 1880 – that 'garage' for horses of gentlemen who had ridden into the city. Among other works, the Penty firm built the Terry Memorial almshouses in Skeldergate in 1899, and a number of streets in the Clementhorpe area of York, before Arthur left the city for London.

THE WELLINGTON INN

Alma Terrace
47 Alma Terrace, Fulford, York YO10 4DL
01904 645642

The Crimea theme continues with the Wellington nearby, unusually situated in the middle of a row of terraced houses in Alma Terrace, off Fulford Road. The pub was originally called the Sir Colin Campbell, named after an officer who fought in the Crimean war at the battle of Alma. Sam Smith brewery bought it in 1887, stripped it of its individual personal name, and it became the Wellington.

Field Marshal Colin Campbell, 1st Baron Clyde, GCB, KCSI (1792–1863) served in the Peninsular War and the War of 1812. He commanded the 98th Regiment of Foot in the First Opium War and then was in charge of a brigade during the Second Anglo-Sikh War. His Highland Brigade distinguished itself at the Battle of Alma in September 1854 (hence the street name) and, with his 'thin red line of Highlanders', Campbell repulsed the Russian attack on Balaclava in October 1854. While the pub name has, sadly, been changed, the street name, happily, remains the same.

BAY HORSE

Fulford
105 Main Street
Fulford York YO10 4PN
01904 633384
www.bayhorsefulford.co.uk

A Bay Horse is recorded in Fulford in 1825, although the present building is from the 1920s. In 1823 Fulford was known as Fulford Gate and was a village in the parish of Fulford Ambo; the population was 182, with two farmers, two blacksmiths, two wheelwrights, two shoemakers, a butcher, a tailor, a shopkeeper, a coal dealer, a corn miller, and the landlords of The Light Horseman, The Saddle, The Board, The Plough, and The Bay Horse public houses. There was also a druggist, a manufacturing chemist, a schoolmaster, nine gentlemen, three gentlewomen, two bankers and seven yeomen.

THE FULFORD ARMS

Fulford
121 Fulford Road, York YO10 4EX
01904 620410
www.thefulfordarms.co.uk

A pub has existed on this site since at least 1822 when it was called the Barrack Tavern and was a vital watering hole for the soldiers at Imphal barracks. Then the pub had a smaller archway and a tobacconists as part of the building. What more could a soldier want?

In 1976 the licensees prudently changed the name of the pub in the wake of the IRA bombings in Strensall and the targeting of buildings linked with the British forces.

THE PLOUGH

Fulford
48 Main Street, Fulford, York YO10 4PX
01904 615431
www.the-plough-inn-York.co.uk

The building is at least 300 years old; records show it serving as The Plough Inn as early as 1822. Before that it was a coach house.

THE SADDLE INN

Fulford
37 Main Street, Fulford, York YO10 4PJ
01904 633317

THE MARCIA INN

Bishopthorpe
29 Main St, Bishopthorpe, York YO23 2RA
01904 706185
www.themarciayork.co.uk

The original name of the village was Thorpe as given in the *Domesday Book*, then Thorpe-on-Ouse in 1194; in 1275 we find Biscupthorpe. In 1202 the monks of St Andrews at Fishergate built the first church here and the name changed to Andrewthorpe, Thorpe St Andrew or St Andrewthorpe; this changed to Bishopthorpe in the 13th century when Archbishop Walter de Grey bought the manor house and presented it to the Dean and Chapter of York Minster. Bishopthorpe Palace was thus born; it has been the residence of the Archbishop of York ever since and is currently the home of Dr John Sentamu. In 1323 a truce was signed here between Edward II and Robert the Bruce after the Battle of Bannockburn. Archbishop Drummond's renovation of the Palace in 1763 produced the Strawberry Gothick west front and gatehouse. In 1832 Reform Bill saw rioters tried to overrun the Palace, incensed by Archbishop Harcourt's lack of support.

The name of the pub derives from the winner of the King's Plate at York in 1802. The pub was once known as the Square and Compasses, the Grey Mare, and the Poacher since 1998, and was the meeting place for the York and Ainsty Hunt. Until 1925 one of the pub's sheds was used as a mortuary for bodies fished out of the Ouse. A sudden change of use was triggered when some children came upon a corpse in the shed.

THE EBOR

Bishopthorpe
46 Main Street, Bishopthorpe, York YO23 2RB

01904 706190

This was formerly the Brown Cow. When Tadcaster Tower breweries sold The Ebor in 1884 it had eight rooms, a dairy and a brewery. Iron and wooden spittoons were included in the sale.

THE WOODMAN

Bishopthorpe
16 Main Street, Bishopthorpe, York YO23 2RB
01904 706507
www.thewoodmaninnpub.com

Bishopthorpe is the setting for *The Lost Luggage Porter* by Andrew Martin, an Edwardian crime novel which uses the old name of Thorpe-on-Ouse. The protagonist, railway detective Jim Stringer, lives on Main Street, Bishopthorpe, and is a staunch patron of the local hostelries, not least the Woodman with its colourful sign and the Ebor, formerly the Brown Cow.

THE SHIP INN

Acaster Malbis
Moor End, Acaster Malbis, York YO23 2UH
01904 703888
www.shipinnacastermalbis.co.uk

Situated on the banks of the River Ouse, Acaster is part-derived from the Latin for camp (*castra*), and is the site of a Roman fort, which was later acquired by an Anglo-Saxon called Aca. After 1066 the manor became the property of the Malbis family. *Domesday* mentions it as 'Acastre'. 'Malbis' is from the Norman Malbysse, or De Malebys, family. Malbis was a Norman personal name which means 'very swarthy'.

THE NAGS HEAD

Askham Bryan
139 Main Street, Askham Bryan, York YO23 3QS
01904 706953

Askham comes from Ascam or Ascha meaning 'enclosure of ash-tree' as given in the *Domesday Book*. It is derived from the Old English pre-7th century 'aesc', ash (tree), with 'ham', settlement or homestead. Bryan was Bryan Fitzalan, son of Scolland, a 12th century owner. Bryan FitzAlan (d. 1 June 1306) was Lord of the Manor of Bedale in Richmondshire, Askham Bryan in the Ainsty, Bainton, Heworth, in Yorkshire, Bicker and Graby in Lincolnshire, a JP, and High Sheriff of Yorkshire. He was a Guardian of Scotland and brother-in-law to King John of Scotland. The village is six miles south-west of York and home to Askham Bryan College of Agriculture. The village has also been called East or Great Askham.

THE ROYAL OAK

Copmanthorpe
1 Main Street, Copmanthorpe, York YO23 3ST
01904 700400

THE THREE HARES INN

Bilbrough
Main St, Bilbrough, York YO23 3PH
01937 918005
www.thethreeharesinn.co.uk

The name Bilbrough means the fortress of the Bila, a pre-Norman Saxon tribe.

The village and the surrounding land was largely the property of the Fairfax family from the 14th century onwards. Thomas Fairfax, parliamentary commander-in-chief during the English Civil War, is buried here in a tomb inside the Fairfax Chapel within the village church.

The village is the subject of *Upon the Hill and Grove at Bilbrough*, written by the 17th century metaphysical poet and politician, Andrew Marvell.

THE BLACKSMITHS ARMS

Naburn
Main St, Naburn, York YO19 4PN
01904 623464
www.blacksmithsarmsnaburn.co.uk

The pub has served the village of Naburn, which has evidence of Saxon and Norman occupation, for some 350 years. There were three alehouses in Naburn in the 1750s and 1760s, but by 1822 only the Horse Shoe remained. In 1872 it was renamed the Blacksmiths Arms; between 1889 and 1901 the publican was also a brewer.

THE FAT ABBOT

Escrick 5www.thefatabbotYork.co.uk

A delightfully named pub set in the grounds of The Parsonage Hotel & Spa. Escrick and the surrounding area had an eventful World War II, situated as it was close to RAF bases at Acaster Malbis and Riccall. Riccall was home to a Heavy Conversion Unit retraining aircrew to fly Halifaxes. Two crashed near Escrick in 1943, killing fifteen crew members in total. Nearby Elvington was the base for Britain's only two Free French bomber squadrons (346 and 347): in 1945 a Halifax taking French aircrew home after the war crashed at Sheepwalk Farm, killing three Frenchmen. The last German plane to be shot down over Britain, a Junkers 88, crashed into a farm at Elvington in March 1945, killing two of the occupants.

THE BLACK BULL

Escrick
Escrick, York YO19 6JP
01904 728245
www.theblackbullescrick.com

THE WHITE SWAN

Deighton
A19, Deighton, York YO19 6HA
01904 728822
www.thewhiteswandeighton@gmail.com

THE WENLOCK ARMS

Wheldrake
73 Main St, Wheldrake, York YO19 6AA
01904 448240
www.thewenlockarms.co.uk

In addition to the Wenlock Arms there was Alice Hawthorne public house (as at Nun Monkton) but this has since been converted into a private house. The pubs were named after a famous racehorse of the 1840s.

ST VINCENT ARMS

Sutton upon Derwent
Main St, Sutton upon Derwent, York YO41 4BN
01904 608349
www.stvincentarms.co.uk

There was at least one alehouse in Sutton in the early 18th century and two or three licensed houses later in the century. In the 19th century by 1823 the Cross Keys and the Ram's Head were up and running. The Ram's Head (replaced by the Clarges Arms by 1840) was renamed the St Vincent Arms by 1879. The St Vincent Arms has mock black beams made from railway sleepers.

Sutton is inextricably linked with the Jervis family, holders of the title of Viscount St Vincent since 1735, when the Manor passed into the hands of Carnegie Robert John Jervis, 3rd Viscount St Vincent in 1857. The family held the Manor until it was sold to the Crown in 1947. Evidence of the Viscount St Vincent association include: the large marble tablet in St Michael's church, commemorating the death of John Edward Leveson Jervis, 4th Viscount St Vincent, in the battle of Abou Klea in Sudan in 1885; the St Vincent Arms; and local streets, St Vincent's Close and Jervis Court.

THE HALF MOON INN

Newton on Derwent
Main St, Newton on Derwent York YO41 4DB
01904 608883
www.thehalfmoonnewton.co.uk

The pub has been here since 1743. A 2014 refurbishment is influenced by O'Reilly's Irish pub in Düsseldorf.

THE GREY HORSE

Elvington
Main Street, Elvington, York YO41 4AG
01904 608335
www.greyhorseelvington.co.uk

The 2015 refit has an aeronautical theme that owes much to the Yorkshire Air Museum, who have provided copies of vintage photographs and helped with some of the air-themed memorabilia on display. The two B&B rooms are named after the Halifax and Buccaneer aircraft – the former having flown from Elvington, and exhibits of the latter are on display at the museum. The upstairs restaurant is The Hangar, with an additional dining room called The Officers' Mess.

The Yorkshire Air Museum is on the site of former RAF Elvington, a Second World War airfield used extensively by Allied bomber crews; it is also the home of The Allied Air Forces Memorial. The museum website tells us that

> Originally a grass airfield, RAF Elvington was completely rebuilt with three hardened runways in 1942, as a sub-station of RAF Pocklington. Grouped with RAF Melbourne, the three airfields became known as '42 Base', within 4 Group. The operational aircraft were Handley Page Halifax four-engined bombers operated by 77 Squadron RAF. The squadron took part in the Battle of the Ruhr and in many other operations aimed at the destruction of the German war industry. In early 1944, 77 Squadron moved to the newly opened airfield at Full Sutton and Elvington became host to two French Air Force Squadrons operating within No. 4 Group: No. 346 (Guyenne) and No. 347 (Tunisie). Both squadrons played a major part in the bomber offensive against Germany. Whilst at Elvington, 77 Squadron lost 82 aircraft and 450 aircrew (comprising Canadians, Australians and New Zealanders as well as British) and this comprised more than half their fatalities during the whole war. No. 77 Squadron lost a total of 883 airman.

THE JEFFERSONS ARMS

Thorganby
Main St, Thorganby YO19 6DA
01904 448316
www.jeffersonarms.co.uk

The Jeffersons Arms – formerly The Indian Elephant restaurant – in Thorganby closed in 2009 but reopened in 2014. Three or four alehouses were licensed in the parish in the 1750s and two later. The Hare and Hounds inn was in the village centre in the 1840s and 1850s but had closed by 1872. The present pub gets its name from Sir John Dunnington-Jefferson, Bt who gifted a building for a village institute in 1921, which was in good use until 1970. The Ferry House or Ferry Boat Inn existed by 1823 and stands near the river. The Smith's Arms, in the village street, was recorded there in the 1840s and 1850s, but had become the Jeffersons Arms by 1872.

THE FERRY BOAT INN

Thorganby
Thorganby, York YO19 6DD
01904 448224

The Ferry Boat Inn was named after the ferry across the Ouse. In 2014 this village pub had been run by the same family for eighty years. The building dates back to the 1700s and was originally the ferryman's house. The pub has been in the family since March 1934. Olive Rogers, landlady in 2014, was one of the longest-serving landladies in the country at the time.

In March 2011 members of the Wheldrake Allotment Society, convening for a meeting in the pub, had a nice surprise when they saw actor Robert Redford and his entourage in The Ferry Boat Inn. Redford was in the UK to promote the four-day Sundance London film festival to be staged in London the following year.

This pub is currently closed.

THE HARE AND HOUNDS
Riccall
8 Silver Street, Riccall, York YO19 6PA
01757 248255
www.wentsfordpubs.com/the-hare-and-hounds

In the later 18th century there was one licensed house in Riccall but by 1823 there were four: the Greyhound, the Drovers' Inn, the Hare and Hounds, and the Shoulder of Mutton. In 1842 there were five public houses dropping back to four in 1851, the Gardeners' Arms replacing the Shoulder of Mutton. After that only the Greyhound, the Hare and Hounds, and the Drovers' Inn are recorded; the last-named apparently closed between 1913 and 1921 while the other two remained.

THE GREYHOUND
Riccall
82 Main St, Riccall, York YO19 6TE
01757 249101
www.thegreyhoundriccall.co.uk

Following close on the heels of the Hare and Hounds is this family-run village pub, which dates back to the late 1800s. The pub has always been popular with cyclists (see the old Cyclists' Touring Club emblem) and walkers using the York–Selby cycle path.

THE FERRY INN
Cawood
2 King St, Cawood, Selby YO8 3TL
01757 268515
www.ferryinncawood.com

Arthur Mee describes Cawood as 'the Windsor of the North' in his *King's England*. Before the Reformation, the Archbishops of York resided here. The name Cawood is reputedly derived from the noise made by local crows in the nearby woods. The village used to have its own gasworks – maybe Mee didn't see it. At one time Cawood supported eighteen pubs – only three are left: The Jolly Sailor, The Ferry Inn and The Castle.

The inn dates back to the 17th century when the only way across the river was by ferry; hence The Ferry Inn. Dick Turpin forded the river here on his escape to York. Cawood Bridge was opened in 1872. The details for the bridge were agreed among the Ecclesiastical Commissioners in the Commercial Inn in Cawood in November 1869. Although a toll equal to the Selby Bridge toll was agreed, this was a temporary measure and the bridge was toll-free from 1882.

THE JOLLY SAILOR INN

Cawood
5 Market Place, Cawood YO8 3SR
01757 268908
www.jollysailorcawood.co.uk

Affiliated to the pub is the The Jolly Sailor Brewery, a micro brewery located at the Olympia Hotel, Selby.

THE CASTLE INN

Cawood
7 Wistowgate, Cawood, Selby YO8 3SH
01757 242837
www.castleincawood.co.uk

> the celebrated Cardinal Wolsey, after residing here a whole summer, and part of the winter [1530], was arrested at this place, on a charge of high treason, by the Earl of Northumberland, and Sir Walter Welsh. The Earl had orders to conduct him to London, for trial, but his death at Leicester, on his journey, terminated the business.
>
> (Letters and Papers, Foreign and Domestic, Henry VIII, Volume 4. 6720; State Papers of Henry VIII Volume 7. 212)

In so doing he fulfilled Knaresborough's Mother Shipton's prophecy that he would see the towers of York Minster but would never be enthroned there.

Four archbishops died here: William Melton in 1340, Cardinal John Thoresby in 1373, William Zouche in 1352 and Thomas Rotherham (of the plague) in 1500. Over the years it was much visited by royalty: for example, King John, for the hunting in Bishop's Wood in the thirteenth century; and Henry VIII and Catherine Howard.

Cardinal Wolsey is reputed to be Humpty Dumpty. Other explanations have Humpty as Richard III, a 'tortoise' siege engine at the Civil War Siege of Gloucester, and a cannon at the Siege of Colchester in 1648.

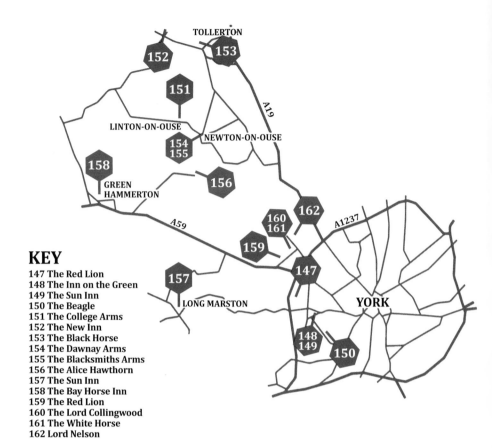

IN THE VILLAGES: WEST

THE RED LION

Knapton
Main Street, Knapton, York YO26 6QG
01904 793957
www.redlionpubYork.com

THE INN ON THE GREEN (formerly Britannia)

Acomb
3 The Green, Acomb, York YO26 5LL
01904 790090
www.innonthegreenacomb.co.uk

The pub name changed from the Britannia in 2013. Acomb, a suburb of York, derives from the Anglo-Saxon Akum, which means oaks, '-um' is an Anglo-Saxon plural. Acomb pre-dates the Norman Conquest and was owned by the Dean and Chapter of York Minster. In the *Domesday* book, the name appears as both Achum and Acum; later variants include Achu, Acun, Akum and Acham. In the 13th century, we find Acome, Acorn and Akome; Akam and Acombe turn up in the 15th century. The three *Domesday* entries are as follows:

> In Achum 14½ carucates for geld, and 8 ploughs can be. St. Peter [the site of the future York Minster] had, and has for 1 manor. 14 rent payers are there now, having 7 ploughs. 6 acres of meadow. Underwood 2 furlongs in length and 2 in breadth. TRE [Tempore Regis Eduardi, in the time of King Edward (the Confessor)it was worth 30 s [shillings]; now the same.

> In Acum Ulchel has 2 carucates of land for geld. Land for one plough. He has half a plough there. Wood 9 furlongs. It is worth 4 s.

> In Acum the Archbishop 14½ carucates. In the same place the King 2 carucates.

An oxgang was the amount of land tillable by one ox in a ploughing season, typically about fifteen acres; a virgate was the amount of land tillable by two oxen in a ploughing season; carucate was the land tillable by a team of eight oxen in a ploughing season.

There is another Acomb near Hexham.

THE SUN INN

Acomb
35 The Green, Acomb, York YO26 5LL
01904 798500
www.thesuninnacomb.com

Previous names for this pub are the Grey Orville, then The Grey Horse right until 1838 when it became the Sun.

THE BEAGLE

Foxwood
169 Foxwood Lane, Foxwood
York YO24 3PG
01904 799701

Converted from a bungalow; opened in December 1977.

THE COLLEGE ARMS

Linton on Ouse
RAF Linton-on-Ouse (HRT), York YO30 2AY
01347 848824

The Manor of Linton was originally owned by the Catholic Appleby family and then bequeathed to University College, Oxford, by a Dr John Radcliffe, Queen Anne's physician, in 1714. He stipulated that the rents raised should pay for scholarships for two medical students. By 1977 the farms, houses and other buildings had reverted to private ownership.

The village is well known for its RAF station and is today the home of No. 1 Flying Training School. During the Second World War it was a bomber base and Squadrons 408 and 426 of the Royal Canadian Air Force, among others, were stationed here. In 1940, after a raid on Cologne, Flying Officer Leonard Cheshire succeeded in getting his badly damaged Whitley bomber back to Linton, for which he was awarded the first of his three DSOs.

THE NEW INN

Tholthorpe
Flawith Rd, Tholthorpe, York YO61 1SL
01347 838329
www.thenewinntholthorpe.co.uk

The pub is unusual because it incorporates a village shop. The other pub, the Plough Inn, is long gone.

Tholthorpe is perhaps best known for its Second World War RAF station and, in particular, for the Canadian squadrons that flew Halifaxes and Lancasters from here from June 1943.

Altogether, 119 Halifax bombers were lost from Tholthorpe, commemorated by the monument there made from Canadian granite. There is also an avenue of oaks and maples, which leads from the village green to the airfield in honour of the fallen airmen.

THE BLACK HORSE

Tollerton
Newton Road, Tollerton, York YO61 1QT
01347 838280

The name Tollerton derives from the village's position at one of the toll entrances to the Forest of Galtres where, according to Verstegan, travellers were, for a fee, given an armed guide to escort them on their journey to Bootham Bar, York. Gill, in his *Vallis Eboracensis*, adds 'it [the forest] was the lurking place of large hordes of banditti, who dwelt in caves and lived upon rapine and plunder'. In the seventeenth century the village was famous for horse racing on land close to the Great North Road. Drunken Barnaby, a celebrated road writer, tells us:

> Thence to Towlerton, where those stagers,
> Or horses courses run for wagers;
> Near to the highway the course is,
> Where they ride and run their horses.

THE DAWNAY ARMS

Newton-on-Ouse
York YO30 2BR
01347 848345
www.thedawnayatnewton.co.uk

The Dawnay Arms, built in 1779, is in Newton-on-Ouse, at the gates to Beningbrough Hall. The garden to the rear stretches down to the River Ouse. Like the pub of the same name in Shipton, it formed part of the Beningbrough Estate, which was owned first by the Bourdner and then the Dawnay families. Features include a river-view dining room, low beams, stripped masonry, open fire, chunky pine tables and old pews on bare boards and flagstones and fishing memorabilia. Goodmanham Brewery beers here have included Randy Monk, Choirboy's Dread and Filthy Habit.

There is a third Dawnay Arms at West Heslerton near Malton.

THE BLACKSMITHS ARMS

Newton-on-Ouse
Cherry Tree Avenue, York YO30 2BN
01347 848249

Nun Monkton

THE ALICE HAWTHORN

Nun Monkton
The Green, Nun Monkton, York
YO26 8EW
01423 330303
www.thealicehawthorn.com

The Alice Hawthorn Inn has stood on Nun Monkton's green village for over 220 years. The Anglo-Saxon name for the village is Monechtone; the eighteen-acre green is one of England's largest and one of the last working greens in Yorkshire; in keeping with the name of the pub, livestock still graze contentedly there.

The old pub is named after one of the greatest English race mares we have known. Born in 1838, Alice Hawthorn won fifty-one races (and ran one dead heat) out of seventy-one races and was placed in ten others in just five seasons including two victories at the Doncaster Derby and Queen's Vase Cup. She won fourteen other cups and eighteen queen's plates; you can find paintings of this 'Queen of the turf' around the pub. The pub was originally called The Inn and then The Blue Bell. There were at least three pubs in the village in the past: The White Horse was opposite on the other side of the green where White Horse House now stands.

An alternative derivation of the name holds that one day a locally bred horse was in difficulties foaling and was helped out by a young girl walking down by the river. The owner of the horse, grateful that she had managed to save the foal, asked the girl to name the horse. She could not think of an appropriate name, other than her own name – Alice Hawthorn. A less romantic derivation has us believe that Alice was the name of the landlord's mistress and the foal was born under a hawthorn bush.

To commemorate the foal, the pub took on this more interesting name, The Alice Hawthorn Inn. Her foals also went on to become Derby winners themselves. The Alice Hawthorn Inn has remained open for over 200 years, except for two years, between 2007 and 2009, when it was closed for a sensitive restoration.

There are numerous pubs named after famous racehorses: Yorkshire alone has more than thirty, some open, some closed. To name but a few, there was another Alice Hawthorn in Wheldrake near York; The Barefoot (closed) in York; Charles XII (of Sweden) at Heslington, York who had to run the 1839 St Leger twice after a dead heat and then walk home from York to Doncaster. There is a Beeswing in York. York too had The Winning Post, The Gimcrack Hotel – the Gimcrack is a race at

An old turnstile used at York racecourse in one of the Alice Hawthorn outhouses.

York in turn named after the horse which won twenty-seven of his thirty-six races over seven seasons; he won his last race in 1771, age eleven and is celebrated in George Stubbs' famous painting. There was also in York The Knavesmire and The Chase, which sported an eight-feet saddle on its sign.

The Chase with its huge saddle.

The Bay Horse (now Keystones) in Monkgate was probably once The Bay Malton named after a horse that flourished between 1764 and 1767. Eclipse (formerly The Black Horse), Old Ebor in Nunnery Lane, Tam O' Shanter in Lawrence Street (although, as stated, it may have something to do with Burns' poem) and The Froghall in Layerthorpe complete our York line-up. Some say the Bay Malton refers to the Bay Horse in Blossom Street.

THE SUN INN

Long Marston
York Road, Long Marston, York YO26 7PG
01904 738258

Undoubtedly, the most famous visitor to this pub would have been Oliver Cromwell, around the time of the famous and decisive Civil War battle at Marston Moor in 1664. The pub itself is named after Edward VI, and has a long been populated by ghosts, which include Cromwell himself, lots of Royalist troops and Prince Rupert of the Rhine fleeing on horseback.

This is very much in keeping with the general supernatural reputation of the area: one website (Ghanon) has the following case report:

> many people have claimed to have seen solid figures limping along the ditches at the roadside, possibly those of the wounded soldiers. A horseman has been seen galloping through the field on the north side and one witness claims that they were chased by the horseman! Figures fighting have been seen down what is known as 'Bloody Lane' and it is said the sounds of the battle can also be heard in the adjourning fields. There has been various activity reported around the supposed 'burial pit' and the distant Elstrop Wood is known as the 'haunted woods' where many soldiers were massacred.

THE BAY HORSE INN

Green Hammerton
York Rd, Green Hammerton, York YO26 8BN
01423 330338

The Hammerton Hotel on the A59 was built as a road house by Bentley Breweries of Leeds in the early 1930s. It was bought by the Bensons in 1992 and converted into the furniture store, which remains today. In 1861 there were four pubs in the village: the Sun, the Railway Tavern, the Rose and Crown Inn and the Victoria. Up until the 1970s Bensons also had a shop, called the Adams House, in Petergate, York.

Green Hammerton is famous for three characters: Alleluia Tommy, real name Thomas Segmore, a prominent Methodist, who lived here; Dick Turpin who lodged here on his way to York; and Wishy Watson who habitually slept in a tree at the north end of the green.

THE RED LION

Upper Poppleton
Boroughbridge Road,
Upper Poppleton, York YO26 6PR
01904 781141
www.redlioncountryinn.co.uk

The Poppleton water pump still can be seen today on the green, close to the maypole. It was probably Poppleton's Red Lion that John Wesley visited in 1743. At this time the landlord was a Charles Hodgson, hence Hodgson Lane. Wesley's diary entry for 18 February that year reads: 'We enquired at Poppleton, a little town three miles beyond York, and hearing there was no other town near, thought it best to call there.' The inn was also called the Four Mile Post and Poppleton House at various times.

THE LORD COLLINGWOOD

Upper Poppleton
The Green, Upper Poppleton, York YO26 6DP
01904 787461
www.lordcollingwood.com

The Lord Collingwood was named after Vice Admiral Cuthbert Collingwood (1748–1810) an admiral in the Royal Navy, and a colleague of Lord Nelson's in several of the British victories in the Napoleonic Wars. On Nelson's death at Trafalgar Collingwood assumed the command of the British fleet. The Lord Collingwood, opposite the green, dates from 1823. Collingwood himself was killed at Toulon in 1810 and is buried in St Paul's Cathedral.

THE WHITE HORSE

Upper Poppleton
The Green, Upper Poppleton, York YO26 6DG
01904 606921
www.whitehorse-poppleton.com

This pub was built in the 1900s.

LORD NELSON

Nether Poppleton
9 Main Street, Nether
Poppleton, York YO26 6HS
01904 794320

The Lord Nelson building was a former farmhouse and is some 300 years old.

The Fox Inn in Church Lane started life on the other side of Church Lane, or Town Street, in around 1822; in 1898 the licence was transferred to premises extending down to the River Ouse. The new building was demolished in 1965 and rebuilt, only to close in 1997.

SOME 21ˢᵀ CENTURY YORK BARS

It is impossible to say always when a pub elides into a bar and vice versa, what makes a place where beer, wine and spirits are drunk a bar and not a pub. York, as with pubs, is particularly blessed with a multitude of good bars of individual character. Here is a small selection of those many bars in York city centre – bars, that is, of the hospitality kind.

BRIGANTES BAR & BRASSERIE

114 Micklegate, York YO1 6JX
01904 675355
www.markettowntaverns.co.uk/pub-and-bar-finder/yorkshire/brigantes

Named after the native British tribe, the Brigantes, who dominated much of northern England before the Romans arrived.

BREWDOG YORK

130-134 Micklegate, York YO1 6JX, England
01904 620773
www.brewdog.com/bars/uk/york

Opened in 2016, I'll let the website do the talking:

> We have opened bars in the centre of historic cities before – Edinburgh, Rome, Warsaw to name but three – and yet aside from strolling past the Colosseum, York has a sense of the past that few others can match. Home to the longest medieval walls in Europe it is a place that carries its history with it, and our latest bar is inside those famous defences a hundred yards from one of the iconic gatehouses that served as the entry points to the city … In York the saying goes 'the streets are Gates, the gates are Bars, and the bars are always full'.

How right they are …

JALOU (formerly THE PARISH and TIGER 10)

Micklegate
Micklegate, York YO1 6LG
01904 466502

A marvellous conversion ... here's some pedantry. What was St John's church, Micklegate, is now a bar (in the social and not the York 'gate' sense of the word); it has a tower base dating from the 12th century. The tower was blown down in 1551 in the same storm that damaged the tower of Holy Trinity Micklegate. Part of the north aisle was rebuilt, although most of the current building dates from the 15th century with rebuilding and restoration in 1850 to enable the widening of North Street. Flooding and the rebuilding of Ouse Bridge in 1763 and 1819 made it necessary to raise the floor. The church closed in 1934, saved from destruction by the York Civic Trust to become the York Institute of Advanced Architectural Studies; in 1960 this merged into the new University of York, which in turn used it as an Arts Centre in the 1960s. St John was later sold to become a bar, Jalou. Like any good patron, the bell ropes still hang around the bar causing occasional ringing sounds.

York Colleges Guild of Bellringers had its origins in St John's when they organised ringing on Wednesday evenings at the former church, which at that time was The Institute of Advanced Architectural Studies. The bells at St John's were an ancient ring of six, but they had been re-hung in a new bell frame and on new fittings in 1954.

EVIL EYE LOUNGE

42 Stonegate, York YO1 8AS
01904 640002
www.evileyelounge.com

'Home of the bizzarre [sic], weird and wonderful' says the website. More like 'home of the bizzarre pallet [sic sic]' – see the website for some impressive spelling. The specialist gin shop is wonderful.

SOTANO CHARCUTERIE & BAR

1 Little Stonegate, York YO1 8AX
01904 620230
www.sotano.co.uk

This bar is in between Banyan and Kennedy's. There are lots of gins and lots of beers, and superb Spanish tapas and the like.

WILDES BAR

21 Grape Lane, York YO1 7HU
01904 610370
www.wildeswinebar.co.uk

Mind your head …

THE ATTIC (AT HARLEQUIN'S) GALLERY COFFEE BAR

2 Kings Square, York YO1 8BH
01904 630631

The pub's website says:

> a beer and coffee enthusiast's dream and offers … an extraordinary
> selection of the world's finest single estate coffee, great regionally
> sourced food, and craft beer from around the world awaits you. A must
> see quirky venue, proud to support local artists.

DYLS CAFÉ BAR

The Motor House Skeldergate Bridge, York YO1 9WJ
www.dylsyork.co.uk

This bar is named after the owner Jan Dyl, and a great little café bar. The castle-like
building here was a toll house; the fee to cross, up to 1914 when tolls were ended,
was 1/2d. Work on the bridge began in 1875; it opened in 1881 at a cost of £56,000
– 40 per cent over budget, replacing the ferry that was used by around 800 people
each day. The bridge had an opening mechanism that has now been immobilised
and is replaced by the bar. *Skeldergate* is from the Norse skjaldari, Shield Makers
Street. The first British case of the 1826 Bengal pandemic was in Sunderland in
September 1831 reaching York in June 1832 at Hagworm's Nest off Skeldergate.

PLONKERS

5 Cumberland Street, York YO1 9SW
01904 655307
www.plonkerswinebar.com

A daft name but a good bar close to the Grand Opera House.

2014 Flooding at Plonkers with the world's press in attendance.

THE STONE ROSES BAR

4 King Street, York YO1 9SP
01904 670696
www.simoncrossleydesign.com

The pub's website tells us it is 'a place that harks back to the golden age of Indie and Britpop – and lots of music related paraphernalia adorn the walls'. The great décor was originally created by Simon Crossley.

YORK THEATRE ROYAL

St Leonard's Pl, York YO1 7HD
01904 623568

Al fresco drinking in 1970 at the Theatre Royal.

THE GUEST PUB

HALES BAR

1-3 Crescent Road, Harrogate HG1 2RS
01423 725 570
http://www.halesbar.co.uk

One of, if not *the* most historic and oldest pubs in Harrogate, Hales Bar is the town's only traditionally gaslit bar. Its origins hail as far back as the earliest days of the town's rise as a leading spa resort and it was one of the first inns to cater for spa visitors after sulphur wells were first established in the mid-17th century. Sulphur springs still bubble beneath the cellar and their unmistakeable smell occasionally percolates up to the bar area.

There are records from the 17th century to inns close to the Old Sulphur Well, mostly from the Pannal Constable, who noted that he went to 'sulfer wells to cease quarrels'; probably it was the Bell, Promenade and White Hart Inns that were implicated in this pubbish disorder.

One of the original gas lighters still working in Hales, courtesy and © Amanda J Wilkinson/CAMRA

The Bell and Promenade Inns were in existence at the time of the 1778 Award, which divided up the Royal Forest; both were tenanted by Joseph Hogg, and the map of the Award depicts a small building on the site of the Promenade Inn. The name Promenade appears in 1822, associated with the neighbouring Promenade Room, now the excellent Mercer Art Gallery, built in 1805–1806. Hales Bar took over the licence of the Promenade when the latter closed in 1840 and was bought by the brewer and developer Thomas Humble Walker for £1,220. Mr Walker extended the old Promenade Inn during the 1840s: the older building was converted into a house, the newer part became an inn that initially took the name of the new landlord, Hodgson. In about 1882, Hodgson was replaced by William Hale.

The old Promenade is often called a coaching inn but there are no records of any coaches stopping there. The confusion may arise from the inn's proximity to the Promenade Coaching Office behind the Bell Inn, from where the coaching companies operated.

The main saloon bar preserves the Victorian atmosphere well, with mirrors and other interesting features and fittings from Victorian days, including those traditional gas lighting and cigar lighters. Tobias Smollett most certainly drank here when in May 1766 he visited Harrogate – the setting for part of his novel *The Expedition of Humphry Clinker*. Hales was a favourite too of Sir John Barbirolli when the Hallé Orchestra was in town; some interior scenes for *Chariots of Fire* were set here.

Refurbishment in 2013 exposed some original beams and stonework, which have been left open to view.

BREWING IN YORK

York has a rich and successful brewing heritage with a number of companies involved in the business of beer brewing down the years.

It wasn't just specialist brewers who made beer. In 1780 John Dale's Bleasdale Ltd was established, which was a manufacturing and wholesale chemist behind Colliergate. A visitor to the firm in the 1930s leaves us with the following description: 'after traversing a dark corridor, found ourselves confronted by a locked door – the entrance to the Poison Rooms. For the first time in my life I saw samples of raw opium – and very disinteresting they looked'.

He would also have seen barrels of black beer, cod liver oil and machinery for grinding liquorice, trimming rhubarb and grinding poppies. Other pharmaceutical and chemical manufacturers included Wright & Prest in Pavement, Edward Wallis & Son in Bedern and Thomas Bishop at North Street Postern. There was also Raimes & Company from 1818 in Micklegate and Henry Richardson & Company, fertilizer makers founded in 1824 at Skeldergate Postern in Clementhorpe.

S.J. Dalton & Company was a mineral water manufactory with beer and stout bottling vaults in Skeldergate. Mr Dalton previously was a senior employee at Savory & Moore, London – chemists to Her Majesty the Queen. D. Moore was another mineral water manufacturer in Backhouse Street, the Groves, established in 1816 and specialising in horehound beer. Their dandelion stout and hop bitters won gold medals at the York Exhibition in 1896. Forster & Taylors in Dale Street off Nunnery Lane were also aerated water manufacturers with beer brewing too no doubt.

In 1835 George Hutchinson took over the Crown at 63 Walmgate (formerly the Crown & Cushion) and started brewing there in what he called the Crown Brewery; their London Brown Stout was popular. Hutchinson later expanded to 27 Pavement.

Yorkshire Clubs Brewery was in New Lane, Huntington. The Loco Brewery moved from Chapmangate, Pocklington, in 1934 into their purpose-built factory in Huntington. Up to fifty workers were employed, some of whom were housed in a row of houses called Brewery Cottages, which survive to this day along with the iron railings that were in front of the brewery building. The brewery vehicles during the Second World War had their headlamps masked (so that they could not be seen by German air crew) and mudguards painted white (so that they could be seen by the residents of Huntington) in the blackout. The brewery closed in 1968 and was demolished in 1973.

Breweries were also being run by the Wormald family and Thomas Hartley in the 18th and 19th centuries. In 1830 we hear of Richard Hood & Sons wine and spirit merchants at 93 Micklegate; in 1834 they took over Francis Moss's wholesale and retail seed business to become wine, spirit, hop and deed merchants based in Mint Yard (around the site of St Leonard's hospital) moving to 21 Micklegate in 1851.

Joseph Hillyard was established in 1840 at 16 Low Ousegate (later the site of O'Neil's Bar) by Joseph Hillyard (silversmith) of Skeldergate and James Hillyard

(tea merchant). Joseph took full control as a coffee, tea, wines and spirit merchant. The firm lasted into the 1980s with Hillyard's Wine Lodge at the back of the Ousegate pub and brewery premises.

There were two pubs called the Board in Goodramgate: one that became the Snickleway Arms, the other opened in 1895 as a shop for W.H. Thackwray who took over John March's brewery behind it in Ogleforth in 1880 (pictured) and also went by the name of Thackwray's.

York's biggest brewery was the Ebor Brewery founded by Joseph Hunt in 1834; he was registered as a hop and seed merchant at 2 Monk Bar. By 1851 he was Brewer, Malster, Hop, Seed & Guavo Merchant at 20 Aldwark. Their Ebor Brewery was established in 1895 and in 1904 took over Robert Brogden, Sons Co. along with their sixty or so licensed pubs. Ebor was acquired by Cameron & Co of West Hartlepool in 1954.

Labels for Hunt's twenty-one beers can be seen at http://labology.org.uk/?page_id=2311.

Hunt's also had a lemonade bottling plant in Bedern, just round the corner, and it owned the Ebor Vaults public house. Apparently, the inn served the cheapest beer in York because the barrels were just rolled across the yard and that meant no dray charges.

Where there was beer there was occasional philanthropy. The Hunt Memorial Homes in Fulford were a gift to the local community from a local brewer, Sir John Hunt, in 1954. There are twenty-four cottages housing ten couples and fourteen individuals, together with two staff houses for a nurse and a handy-man.

In the 1950s brewers were Hope & Anchor Hungate; John J. Hunt, Spurriergate; Tadcaster Tower in Piccadilly and the Yorkshire Clubs Brewery in Marygate. *Kelly's Directory* for 1973 reveals the following two brewers: Bass Charrington, Piccadilly; Yorkshire Club's Brewery, Huntington.

In the early 21st century, changing social demographics, business economics, more discerning socialisation and a desire for real tasting beers all conspired to revolutionise the brewing landscape – very much for the better. From now on microbreweries, real ale and craft beers would be all the rage. Here are just a few of York's modern beer makers:

www.rudgatebrewery.co.uk
2 Centre Park, Marston
Business Park, Tockwith,
York YO26 7QF

www.thehopstudio.com
The Hop Studio Ltd, 3
Handley Park, Elvington,
York YO41 4AR

www.treboom.co.uk
Treboom Brewery,
Millstone Yard, Main Street,
Shipton-by-Beningbrough,
York YO30 1AA

www.Yorkshireheart.com
Pool Lane, Nun Monkton
York YO26 8EL

www.brewYork.co.uk
Enterprise Complex,
Walmgate, York YO1 9TT

www.ainstyales.co.uk
Manor Farm Buildings,
Intake Lane, Acaster Malbis,
York YO23 2UJ

In May 2017 a five-day festival of local beers was held at the Fox in Holgate Road. Fifteen small breweries all within twenty-five miles of the Fox stood the drinks for the event: Ainsty Ales of Acaster Malbis; Bad Seed and Brass Castle from Malton; Treboom of Shipton-on-Beningbrough; Rudgate of Tockwith; Brown Cow of Barlow; Jolly Sailor from Selby; Great Heck of Goole; Hop Studio from Elvington; Yorkshire Heart from Nun Monkton; Half Moon from Melbourne, East Yorkshire; Roosters of Knaresborough; Bad Co of Dishforth; and Brew York and York Brewery, both of York.

It comes as no surprise that beer, brewing and inns themselves feature frequently in pub names. There is a Cock and Bottle in York; The Corporation Brewery Taps in Doncaster, The Hogshead at Woodhouse near Sheffield and the amusing Jack and Gill in Allerton. You might have wanted to slip in the tiny Slip Inn north of York (now gone), although the pub of the same name on the city's Ouse refers to the river traffic; failing that, drop in at The Drop Inn in Guisely or go to The Local in Leeds or one of Hull's two Full Measures. Pig and Whistles (as in Pudsey) signify the mug into which your beer was poured from the jug (for example, in Leeds). The Boy and Barrels at Selby and Mexborough is Bacchus, the Roman god of wine sitting on a tun of ale.

TEMPERANCE

In a book that is fulsome in its praise for the English pub it is only right to remember that not everyone in the nation has always been enamoured by inns, taverns and alehouses. Indeed, some eschew such establishments completely and, for various good reasons, avoid beer and other alcoholic beverages. To provide a degree of context and balance it is important to look at temperance and abstinence, especially as it has related to York.

The York Temperance Society was set up in 1830 with forty subscribers and Joseph Rowntree as Secretary; membership grew to nearly 1,000 by 1936 – 3.3 per cent of the city population at this time. The Rowntree family, as Quakers, were prime movers in the drive for temperance. From 1836 there were rival organisations advocating total abstinence and variously called New Temperance, Total Abstinence or Teetotal; an Association of Abstainers started in 1874. The York Temperance Society protested on such issues as the extension of licensing hours to 11.00 p.m., Sunday closing, banning the sale of alcohol to children, and grocers' licences. Members were also instrumental in thwarting licence renewals at The Golden Slipper Inn and The Corporation Arms in Friargate. In Walmgate alone there were twenty inns, according to *White's 1830 Trade Directory*, so convincing people to abstain was nothing if not an upward battle; across the city there was an inn for every twenty-eight families.

The Temperance movement and Quakers were inextricably linked; in May 1850 a meeting of the Friends interested in Temperance was held at the London Yearly Meeting. Members of the provisional committee included James Backhouse and Joseph Spence of York; in August that year a further meeting was held in York to confirm this as a national organisation. *The Yorkshire Herald* reported on the copious statistics provided to outline the extent of the alcohol abuse problem in York: 50,000 gallons of spirits were consumed annually while some York streets, for example Water Lane, were awash with beer and spirit shops – four within the space of just under 100 yards. Noting that there were 302 public houses and dram shops in the city in 1851 – or one for every twenty-six families – Rowntree petitioned the magistrates to grant no more licences. In 1851 it had warned

> beware the necessity of cheap beer, or 'liquid food' for the support and comfort of the working man and the desirableness of affording him every facility of obtaining it ... the Beer Act has done more to demoralize our youthful population and neutralize the labours of the Sabbath School Teacher.

But it was, nevertheless, optimistic: 'light finds its way through the smallest crevice … we already perceive a vast change in the public mind'. The York Band of Hope was set up around 1847 and educated 1,200 children under sixteen in temperance principles and healthy, alcohol free lifestyles; a trip to Moreby Hall, south of York, took 800 children; 3,000 copies of their magazine, *The Visitor*, were regularly distributed. Nationwide, by 1897, the membership was 3,238,323; Queen Victoria became patron in 1897. Sabbatarianism was another cause: Rowntree believed that inebriation, prostitution and gambling were all exacerbated by breaking the Sabbath.

The cholera epidemic of 1831 was thought to have been fuelled by 'intemperance and low living'. On 28 June it had spread to the workhouse in Marygate where it killed eight inmates; by 2 July it had reached all parts of the city. By the end 104 men had died and sixty-nine women, the remainder children. Initially, the *Yorkshire Gazette* reported that the disease only affected people 'in want of cleanliness, habits of intemperance and low living, the consequence of poverty and distress' – in other words, the feckless poor. It described one victim as living in a 'depraved and immoral manner'; another was the wife of a black man, addicted to hard spirits (fourteen glasses a day); another had been 'inebriated for four or five days'. Things had already changed by 9 June, though, when it became obvious that cholera recognised no social or behavioural boundaries. The death from cholera of Ruth Bellerby, a Wesleyan Methodist and sister-in-law of the editor of the *Yorkshire Gazette*, confirmed that beyond all doubt.

In 1851 John Stephenson Rowntree tells us that the Adult Schools were being used as a recruitment vehicle for the Friends' Temperance Society, although they stopped short of imposing total abstinence at the school. A pledge book was provided by the Temperance Society but it failed to attract a single entry. Nevertheless, a temperance society was set up in the school in 1861 and in 1871 Saturday night meetings designed to lure people from the public houses put on readings, singing, panoramic and lantern shows and ventriloquism; a Band of Hope was often heard playing in the school.

In 1841 a Temperance Coffee House had opened in Colliergate changing to The Commercial Temperance Hotel on its move to Low Ousegate in 1843. In 1877 the Society bought a lecture theatre in Goodramgate and renamed it the Victoria Hall.

In York, 1862 was a pivotal year for temperance. It was then that Henry Isaac Rowntree bought the Tukes' cocoa and chocolate business in Castlegate, calling it the 'Cocoa, Chocolate and Chicory Works'. The stimulus may have come from the fact that Joseph Rowntree's existing grocery business in Pavement was already well established and capably run by Henry's brothers, John Stephenson and Joseph Rowntree, who were made partners on reaching their majority; it may also have been triggered by a desire to offer the public a non-alcoholic alternative beverage in keeping with Quaker temperance principles and as pioneered by Joseph Fry in Bristol and then George Cadbury in Bournville. Henry and Joseph shared a belief in, and derived satisfaction from, the knowledge that the production of cocoa was a potent weapon in the battle for temperance and that the well-provisioned alcohol-free shop in Pavement, and the very act of manufacturing cocoa, was an essential service to the community.

Joseph Rowntree was a co-founder of the Temperance Legislation League with Lord Peel and committee chairman until his death. A Yorkshire Quarterly Meeting in 1889 stung him into action when he heard Friends claiming that poverty was accountable solely to 'the drink'. Joseph believed that 'the drink' was a cause but only a contributory cause. To prove this, in the 1890s Joseph Rowntree and Arthur Sherwell published *The Temperance Problem and Social Reform*, although in 1874 records show that Rowntree may not have favoured total abstinence if the invoice for an order for a case of champagne sent to his home was anything to go by. The book was a best seller and went on to sell a huge 70,000 copies in nine editions.

In 1889 York Railway Institute was opened on the back of all this on the site of the Railway Tavern to provide educational and recreational activities for the railway workers of York. It survives and thrives today with over 3,000 members with activities ranging from sailing and golf, judo, dance, pilates, yoga, brass bands and theatre to chess and dominoes. The site was also significant in that it removed one of the temptations open to workers who arrived at their benches after 'a swift half'; there were, of course, many pubs in which to imbibe in the vicinity, but it was a start. Another attempt at spreading temperance came in the shape of mobile Temperance Coffee Wagons shops run by the Quaker York Adult Schools between 1871 and 1880; one was strategically stationed outside the works at Queen Street. 'Mechanics and others going to their labours in the morning' could get coffee to go for ½d a cup Monday to Friday with a meal deal bun at the same price.

One of the coffee carts.

The opening of the original Railway Library and Reading Room Institution was celebrated with a grand tea in the Lecture Hall in Goodramgate with music by the band of the 7th Hussars (ironically, it seems, on a George Hudson scale of grandness). It had as its model the York Institute for Popular Science, Art and Literature and had as its aim to help younger railway employees 'to employ their energies better than by wandering about the streets or resorting to places which would neither improve their minds nor their pockets'. Other such NER Institutes existed by now at Shildon (1833, the world's first), Gateshead (1857), Darlington (1858); Forth (Newcastle), Blyth and Dairycoates (Hull).

Self improvement and education were paramount. In the lofty and somewhat garbled words of George Leeman, the mission statement for the Institute was a place in which 'the men, whose brawny arms and strong muscle and mechanical skill work out that great an important agent of the present century to which this country is indebted for the pre-eminent position it holds in the scale of nations'. To that end the Institute was equipped with a library and a reading room with books, periodicals and York's weekly newspapers; dailies were not published in the city until later in 1874. Initially, most of the books were donated by members, friends and shareholders of the NER mounting to an impressive stock of 9,223 at the closure of the old library in 1889; this formed the basis of the new library which was in the Sack Warehouse in the old station yard. In total, 24,000 loans were issued each year to 512 members.

The subscription for the Institute was 1d a week. The new Institute dining hall seated 400 diners with heating-up facilities for workers who brought breakfast and lunches from home; there was a smoke room 'for those who wished to indulge in the doubtful enjoyment of smoking' and a games room for cards, bagatelle, chess and billiards, and five classrooms, as well as the luxury of lavatories, which the old building never had. The new building continued the mission 'to convey information and spread education on a variety of subjects'. 'Improving subjects' formed the basis of the lectures. A branch of the NER Bank of Deposits opened there. The Institute was to some extent a working man's Assembly Rooms, but with a formal educational aspect.

No alcohol was allowed on the premises, although tea and coffee were in good supply. This comes as no surprise as the founder president, Henry Tennant, was a Quaker and a prominent figure in the NER Temperance Union. However, three years after Tennant's retirement the Institute was clearly leaking members to other non-dry 'clubs' in the city.

The use and abuse of alcohol were to feature prominently as significant causes of poverty in Seebohm Rowntree's landmark, turn of the (20th) century *Poverty: A Study of Town Life*. We owe him much for our understanding of poverty and the impact of alcohol due largely to his rigorous, robust and systematic research techniques. Focussing on the desperate Hungate and Walmgate areas, he describes them as typical of urban slum life: 'reckless expenditure of money as soon as obtained, with the aggravated want at other times; the rowdy Saturday night, the Monday morning pilgrimage to the pawn shop ... the despair of so many social workers'; although he is careful to add that he is all too mindful of the many individual exceptions to the rule where thrift, self-discipline and self respect predominate.

Here are some random examples of the house-by-house research carried out on a street by street basis: typical comments were 'Out of work; drinks, "chucked his work over a row"; very poor; have to pawn furniture to keep children. Rent 4s'. Poverty in Class D (in which the average family size is 4.03 and average weekly earnings are 41s 9¼d, including children's contributions) exists only through 'wasteful expenditure' for, example, on drink and gambling. 'There is no doubt that the average weekly expenditure upon alcoholic drink … is considerable.'

His research introduces evidence from food nutrition specialists and physiologists to establish the calories required by working men and women and the diets that deliver them, before they succumbed to weight loss and illness. One of the nutritionists was Professor W.O. Atwater, a leading expert from the United States Department of Agriculture whose findings he cross-checked against the research of Noel Paton and other British scientists. Ironically for Seebohm Rowntree, Atwater also proved that alcohol generated heat in the human body and could be used as fuel like carbohydrates. This fact was used by the drinks industry in the promotion of alcohol, something that disappointed Atwater greatly, prominent as he was in the temperance movement. He was one of the first nutritionists to prove that Americans ate too much fat and sweets and did not exercise enough.

A supplementary chapter provides statistics on public houses in York (and on the provision of education). Seebohm Rowntree found that in a population of 77,793 people there were 199 fully licensed houses, thirty-seven beerhouses and 102 off licences, which equates to one licensed premise for every 230 people in York; in Walmgate and Hungate the number was that much lower at one for 174 people. Nationally, York was above average with Northampton at 167, and at the other end, Cardiff at 458 and Leeds at 362.

His surveillance (seventeen consecutive hours on a Saturday) of footfall in the typical 'small dingy looking house [pub] in a narrow street in the heart of a slum district' revealed 550 people going in: 258 men, 179 women and 113 children. Seventeen men and twenty-three women made return visits. Morning traffic was no more than eighteen customers per hour while afternoons and evenings were twice that. The busiest times were 9 and 10 p.m. with eighty-three customers, with seventy-four between 10 and 11 p.m. In total, 278 adults came in alone, 90 in couples and 69 in parties of three or more. Of the 258 men, 158 stayed longer than fifteen minutes while only forty-four of the women did likewise. We can glean similar 'business' data today on the internet entry for every pub.

Contemporary police reports show that these public houses 'attracted low-class custom not only from the rest of York and the nearby barracks, but from the surrounding towns and villages', which led to high levels of disorderly behaviour and a proliferation of prostitution in the area – nearly one third of all York's prostitutes worked in Walmgate alone. Seebohm Rowntree's picture of the typical pub, though, is one of 'social attractiveness', which 'struck him very forcibly. It points to the need for the establishment on temperance lines of something equally attractive in this respect'.

> The rooms are, as a rule, brilliantly lit, and often gaudily, if cheaply, decorated. In winter they are always kept temptingly warm. The company is almost entirely composed of young persons, youths and girls, sitting round the room and at small tables. Often there is a considerable number of soldiers present. Every one is drinking, but not heavily, and most of the men are smoking. At intervals one of the company is called on for a song, and if there is a chorus, every one who can will join in. Many of the songs are characterised by maudlin sentimentality; others again are unreservedly vulgar. Throughout the whole assembly there is an air of jollity and an absence of irksome restraint which must prove very attractive after a day's confinement in factory or shop.

The lesson learnt here was the need for social activities that allow people to escape the daily grind, but without alcohol.

Alcohol is, unsurprisingly, a problem too in the findings from the research done by Seebohm Rowntree for the 1951 publication of *English Life and Leisure: A Social Study*. Unenforced leisure as a concept and as a chosen social activity was something quite new – hitherto, it had been solely an obligatory by-product of unemployment. Shorter working hours and longer statutory holidays (pioneered, ironically, to some degree by the Rowntrees) meant that the working man and woman now had time on their hands to do with as they wished. The first print run of 7,500 copies of the book sold out within a few weeks, as did a 2,000-copy reprint. Sales of *English Life and Leisure* exceeded 10,000 by the end of the year; 'Despite the bitter criticism it evoked, both from clerical professionals and lay experts … [it] survived to become an enduring classic of modern British social science'. According to Seebohm Rowntree it was the only book he published that saw a profit.

The intriguing interviews that formed the basis of the book, often somewhat impressionistic and judgmental, are nothing if not frank; they provide a fascinating insight into a new and unexplored stratum of life at the time, as these random selections show:

> Mrs W. is distrustful of her fellow humans for most of them look down on her and show it. She might be any age between 40 and 55, but says she is 39. She is enormously fat, to an extent that defies description, and though she lives in a large, well-fitted council house in a large town, she is a complete slattern. She goes about with her clothes unfastened, bare feet thrust into muddy carpet slippers, long black hair uncombed, dirty hands and dirty face. Two men live with her, to one of whom she is married, and her children are divided between them. She is now pregnant again and it is astonishing that either of the men both decent working-class types could copulate with such a monstrous creature. Mrs. W. herself had her first child at the age of 17 out of wedlock. The child, a girl, in turn had her first child at the age of 17 out of wedlock. Mrs. W. says rather helplessly that she supposes any day now the second daughter will probably come

home and say she is 'in trouble.' Because the neighbours openly scowl at Mrs. W. ('She lets down the neighbourhood') she seldom goes out except for shopping. She is friendly once she gets over her suspicion, and the home is clean although untidy. Mrs. W. is a good cook and a devoted though not very prudent mother. She drinks spirits heavily when she can afford them (in this ménage à trois there is plenty of money), and smokes heavily. She never goes to church because, she says, when she was a kid and first 'in trouble' and needed a bit of help, the church people were the first to turn their noses up at her. Now she doesn't want anything to do with them.

Overcrowding under the looming shadow of Leethams mill.

Squalor in Wray's Yard, Hungate made worse with flooding.

On the other hand:

> Mrs D. is a young housewife of 26. Her husband is an architect. They are very much in love and are anxious to get a house of their own (they are now in a furnished flat) because they want to start a family. They hope to have three children. Mrs. D. is a very gentle person who would do anything for anyone. She has not been a regular churchgoer but was married in church and has started going occasionally. As far as can be told, her life has no vice or unpleasantness of any kind, and a church could hardly make her better! She is a teetotaller and non-smoker. Is of course innocent sexually, and does not gamble. She likes the radio, cinema and theatre, but her main recreation is looking after her husband.

We hear also of Mr H, twenty-two year old son of a publican who 'smokes heavily and considers himself something of a Don Juan, has no discernible interests except gambling, women and drink ... a nasty piece of work'. Other chapters follow on 'Drink' where we learn that

> the total personal expenditure on alcoholic beverages in 1948 was £762 million, compared with 285 million in 1938 ... the nation was spending: (a) one-quarter more on alcohol than the total spent on rent, rates and water charges; (b) more than five and a half times as much on alcohol as on books of all kinds, and on newspapers and magazines; (c) seven shillings on alcohol for every £ spent on food.

Flawed as it may be in certain aspects, its merit lies in the fact that it shines new light into an area of British life that hitherto had been scarcely examined but which, at the dawn of the television age, was an increasingly important aspect of our society.

In 1929 there were three temperance hotels in York: The Minster Commercial in St Martin's Crescent off Micklegate; Frank's at 134 Micklegate, Sanderson's Temperance Hotel, Goodramgate and Young's Private & Commercial at 24 High Petergate.

Goodramgate: to the right is Sanderson's Temperance Hotel.

Here is some other evidence of temperance activity in York:

Lady Peckitt's Yard Chapel: the Wesleyan Methodists laid the foundation stone in 1829. In 1936 seven people here signed the total abstinence pledge and formed the basis of the York Temperance Society. It was sold in 1874 to the Adult School Movement who built a school there; Sarah Rowntree laid the foundation stone in 1875.

Swedenborgians were first recorded in York between 1790 and 1800. From 1855 to 1876 they used the Temperance Lecture Hall in 46 Goodramgate, known earlier as Sanderson's Temperance Hotel; it has now been demolished.

Wesleyan Protestant Methodism was introduced into 1829 with 230 Wesleyan Methodists who initially met in a room behind the Old Sand Hill public house (now demolished) in St Andrewgate.

The Congregationalist Chapel, Walmgate, opened in 1824 in a passage near the Admiral Hawke public house. It was closed before 1850 after the Wesleyan Reformers had been using it and is now demolished.

In November 1781 the Grape Lane Chapel between Grape Lane and Coffee Yard was built and occupied for two years until, in 1798, it was sold to the Methodist New Connexion. When, in 1796, part of the Grape Lane Chapel congregation seceded, they moved into a small, newly built chapel in Upper Jubbergate, Jubbergate Chapel. In the mid-19th century when occupied by the Primitive Methodists, Grape Lane was by all accounts now a thoroughly damp, miserable, whore-ridden and cheerless place; in 1821 according to Camidge, himself a Primitive Methodist, the congregation was bullied and victimised:

> on some Sundays men went to the services accompanied by dogs which they had kept short of food for two or three days ... as soon as the preacher started to speak, one of them would throw a bone onto the chapel floor. The dogs were let loose and the fight for the bone generally lasted long enough to destroy the whole service. Sometimes the men would carry sparrows in their pockets and ... set them free so that they blundered against the candles, putting them out. At other times they would contradict the preacher, or begin a mock service of their own. If denied admission they would fire brimstone and cayenne pepper through the keyhole ... on occasions they fired powder and homemade crackers, or fastened the chapel doors from the outside.

(William Camidge, *Primitive Methodism* 1901)

The Bloomsbury public house next door cannot have helped matters. A timely visit by the Lord Mayor one evening ended the abuse and disruption. Grape Lane Chapel was demolished in 1963.

The earliest temperance societies were inspired by Belfast professor of theology, and Presbyterian Church of Ireland minister John Edgar, who famously poured his stash of whisky out of his window in 1829. Joseph Livesey underwrote his philanthropic work in temperance with the profits he made from cheese production. The word teetotal comes from a speech by Richard (Dickie) Turner, a follower of Livesey, in Preston in 1833: 'I'll be reet down out-and-out t-t-total for ever and ever.'

Livesey opened the first temperance hotel in 1833 and the next year founded the first temperance magazine, *The Preston Temperance Advocate* (1834–1837). The British Association for the Promotion of Temperance was established by 1835 and had as its mission statement 'Education for all'. A contemporary pamphlet urges residents to 'come as you are, do not stoop to black your boots'.

In 1847, the Band of Hope was founded in Leeds, the aim of which was saving working class children from the perils of drink. The members were obliged to pledge to abstain 'from all liquors of an intoxicating quality, whether ale, porter, wine or ardent spirits, except as medicine'.

In 1853, the Maine law in the US inspired the United Kingdom Alliance – a hard-line group of prohibitionists – to advocate, divisively, a similar law prohibiting the sale of alcohol in the UK. This was opposed by less radical temperance organisations who preferred moral persuasion to a legal ban. The impotence of legislation in this field became all too clear when the Sale of Beer Act 1854, which restricted Sunday opening hours, had to be repealed, following widespread rioting. In 1859 a prototype prohibition bill was overwhelmingly defeated in the House of Commons.

A breakthrough came in the shape of Norman Shanks Kerr who promoted the *treatment* of inebriates and held that inebriety was a disease, not a vice. In 1884, in response to the inadequacy of the Habitual Drunkards Act of 1879, he founded the Society for the Study and Cure of Inebriety and was the first president; the society still exists as the Society for the Study of Addiction.

Nathaniel Currier (1813–1888) and James Merritt Ives (1824–1895) produced over thirty prints that focussed graphically on the Temperance Movement. This one shows a semi-circle of male figures beginning with Step 1. 'A glass with a Friend' up and over semi-circle to Step 9 'Death by suicide'. Half circle bottom centre with an image of a weeping woman walking with a child.

'*Steps*: 1. A glass with a friend 2. A glass to keep the cold out 3. A glass too much 4. Drunk and riotous 5. The Summit attained; Jolly Companions; a confirmed drunkard 6. Poverty and disease 7. Forsaken by friends 8. Desperation and crime 9. Death by suicide.'

William Meacham Murrell's equally evocative 1846 Map of Temperance. The website tells us that it is 'An early allegorical map on temperance, accompanied by a lengthy poem. Typical of "didactic" visual aids intended to be "at once entertaining and instructive". … colorful and intricate temperance maps depicting the "Ocean of Life" trained viewers to see that the path to damnation was … a veritable riptide towing the sinner from the first sip of grog to the channel of destruction. The apparent innocuousness and swift danger of water made it a potent metaphor for life's temptations in an era when waterways were primary transportation routes, and accidental drownings and shipwrecks not uncommon. The maps vividly showed that "Religion Channel" was just one strong current away from "Misery Regions" and the "Reprobate Empire", not only for seasoned tipplers but for all on the "Ocean of Life".'
(www.digital.library.cornell.edu/catalog/ss:3293739)

Secular temperance organisations connected to the labour movement started to emerge, for example the Scottish Prohibition Party, founded by a communist temperance activist called Bob Stewart – a Marxist offshoot called the Prohibition and Reform Party, which later became part of the Communist Party of Great Britain in 1920.

The former Manchester City FC football stadium, Maine Road, gets its name from a renaming of Dog Kennel Lane by members of the Temperance Movement, inspired by the 1853 Maine law.

Religion played a part: various Nonconformist groups – the Methodists, Quakers and The Salvation Army (founded 1864), lobbied Parliament to restrict alcohol sales. In Wales, Lady Llanover, motivated by Calvinistic Methodists teachings, closed all the public houses on her estate and was an outspoken critic of the evil drink. The Church of England Temperance Society was founded in 1862; its volunteers in the court system led to the first probation service. The League of the Cross was a Catholic total abstinence organisation founded in 1873 by Cardinal Manning. In 1876 the British Women's Temperance Association was formed to persuade men to stop drinking, rebranded in 2006 as the White Ribbon Association.

The battle for temperance, then, was hard fought; it may be that those who fought the fight believed that if only one drinker was dissuaded from the drink then the arduous fight was well worth it. In the event, it is estimated that in 1900 10 per cent of the adult population was teetotal. That must be considered a success. At the same time, we know that beer drinking was on the decline with 138 pubs calling time for the last time.

The pub was not helped by the First World War, during which it was standard practice for (mainly male) workers in restricted occupations to have a drink before work and in the lunch break. This had a detrimental effect on productivity, particularly in munitions; so bad was it that David Lloyd George said in February 1915 when querying the reasons behind the shortfall in output: 'let us be perfectly candid. It is mostly the lure of the drink … drink is doing more damage in the war than all the German submarines put together'.

So, in passing the Defence of the Realm Act in 1914 the Liberal Government gave temperance an unexpected boost: pub hours were reduced, beer was watered down and was subject to a penny a pint extra tax; the momentum was maintained by the subsequent State Management Scheme in 1916, which nationalised breweries and pubs in certain areas of Britain where armaments manufacture was taking place. In 1931 a Royal Commission was able to declare that getting drunk had gone out of fashion; in modern parlance, it was no longer cool.

INTEMPERATE DRINKING IN YORK

York, like anywhere else, has some epic stories to tell about the effects of ale on some of its drinkers. Here are just a few examples from York's annals of alcohol abuse.

Jucundus the Monk – party animal

When Jucundus joined the 15th century monks of St Leonard's Hospital he was making a mistake – the well-named novice was rather bibulous and something of a party animal. His chosen life of asceticism did not sit well with him, so he compromised and decided to live a life of austerity all year long – apart from on one day. This day happened to coincide with York Fair – never an abstemious event – to which Jucundus repaired and truly let down what was left of his hair. The following day he was wheeled home in a barrow and tried by the authorities for his decadence and permissiveness – his punishment was to be walled up without delay in the Priory cellar.

Immuration was fairly low down on Jucundus's list of things to do before he died; his physical struggle to save himself resulted in the wall collapsing, through which he tumbled into St Mary's Abbey immediately next door. He soon became a Benedictine monk there and a paragon of sobriety.

One year or so later Jucundus was appointed keeper of the cellar; unfortunately, this cellar contained wine and, soon after his appointment, Jucundus was found comatose at the wrong end of a barrel of claret: his punishment was, again, to be immured at the scene of the crime – which happened to be the exact place through which Jucundus had tumbled from the priory next door. As before, Jucundus was not going to take this lying down, or even walled up. His former colleagues in the priory heard the commotion he made, tore down the walls and were confronted by the miracle that was Jucundus. So stupefied where they that they made Jucundus Prior of St Leonard's.

This story, though apocryphal, does make the point that the monasteries were among the first brewers of ale for mass public consumption, running as they did hostels or guest houses for travellers and pilgrims. No doubt there was some private consumption going on …

In the Middle Ages there was a Taverners' or Vintners' Guild in York, and in the 14th century at least thirty of them were admitted as Freemen of the City, including the Brewer of St Leonard's Hospital.

The Great Feast of Cawood

The Great Feast of Cawood was held to celebrate the enthronement of George Nevill as Archbishop of York in 1466. His brother, the Earl of Warwick, the 'Kingmaker', organised it to include:

> 104 oxen, six wild bulls, 1,000 sheep, 304 veal, 304 pigs, 400 swans, 2,000 geese, 1,000 capons, 104 peacocks, 400 mallards and teals, 204 cranes, 204 kids, 2,000 chickens, 4,000 pigeons, 4,000 conies, all washed down with 25,000 gallons of wine and 62,000 gallons of ale.

What was that about gluttony being one of the seven deadly sins?

'Colourful Nocturnal Habits'

For the thirty-six Vicars Choral of York Minster Bedern Chapel was their first home from 1349. The covered way over Goodramgate was allowed by Richard II and made it easy for the vicars to get to the Minster, avoiding the 'common people'. The present chapel dates from 1370 and was used until 1650 after which time in the 19th century it became a 'sad spectacle of poverty and wretchedness' when divided into slum tenements, largely for Irish navvies. The priests in Bedern had been indulging in 'colourful nocturnal habits' and were re-housed in St William's College so that their behaviour could be monitored more closely. It seems reasonable to assume that immoderate alcohol consumption was one of those 'colourful nocturnal habits'. One incident involved one of the cathedral freelances hitting a man over the head with (the blunt end of) an axe.

Mutton Curry – Dipsomaniacal Hangman

York always had its own hangman in the 18th century, appointed from the inmate population. Between 1802 and 1835, John (or William) Curry, or Curry Wilkinson officiated at the Knavesmire. He was known as 'Mutton Curry' because he had twice been convicted of sheep stealing, having had his death sentence at the Knavesmire commuted on each occasion. On the second occasion, he was awaiting transportation when the post of hangman became vacant and he accepted it. His first assignment was (ironically) hanging three men on the 28 August 1802 for stealing sheep, cattle and from a dwelling house, respectively.

By 1810 he had performed twenty-five executions, including a number of convicted Luddites from Cartwright's Mill at Rawfolds, as described in Charlotte Bronte's 1849 *Shirley*. In all, Curry was responsible for at least sixty-three verifiable executions during his thirty-three-year reign, which ended with a triple execution on Monday 6 April 1835, when Ursula Lofthouse, Joseph Healy and William Allott were hanged for murder. Lofthouse had murdered her husband.

All did not always go well though: as a convicted felon, Curry remained a prisoner himself until 1814. He found his job stressful and took to drinking a lot of gin to steel himself for the task at hand. On 14 April 1821, he was called upon to perform two executions. First he hanged highwayman Michael Shaw at York Castle and then had to walk across town to execute William Brown for burglary at the City Gaol. He was somewhat drunk by the time he got there and while waiting on the platform for the prisoner to appear, he began shaking the noose at rowdy spectators, calling out to them: 'Some of you come up and I'll try it!' The crowd was furious and cried 'shame; he's drunk!' When Brown appeared, Curry had to be assisted by a warder and one of the Sheriff's officers.

A report in *The Times* of 24 April 1821 said:

> The executioner, in a bungling manner and with great difficulty (being in a state of intoxication), placed the cap over the culprit's face and attempted several times to place the rope round his neck, but was unable. He missed the unfortunate man's head with the noose every time that he tried. The cap was each time removed from the malefactor's face, who stared wildly around upon the spectators.

The *Times* reported that the crowd were not amused by this and called out, 'Hang him, hang Jack Ketch' (the generic name for the hangman).

On 1 September 1821, Curry was booked to hang five men at one time. The execution was reported by *The Yorkshire Gazette* as follows.

> On Saturday last, a few minutes before 12 o'clock, the unfortunate men were conducted from their cells to the fatal drop. After a short time spent in prayer they were launched into eternity. None of them seemed to suffer much. However, by an unaccountable neglect of the executioner (Curry) in not keeping sufficiently clear of the drop when the bolt was pulled out, he fell (into the trap) along with the malefactors.

Curry retired, twenty hangings later, *otium sine dignitate* to the Thirsk Poor House in 1835. *The Yorkshire Gazette* pointed out that 'gin was apt to provide a snare for him'.

The Rowntree Office Day Out

Joseph Rowntree instituted the work's outing at his firm, intended, no doubt, as a bonding exercise. One such trip was perhaps a little too bonding and something of a disaster, particularly when viewed from a Quaker temperance standpoint. On a day out from York to Whitby, some of the more enterprising members of the party left their chartered train at Goathland intending to walk the rest of the way and meet the main group for an afternoon stroll along the beach. Rain intervened and diverted the walkers into a public house for 'shelter'; many emerged much the worse for drink and had to be escorted back to the station by the police. Needless to say, there were no more outings for a while.

Pavement – The Micklegate Run of the 19th Century

With alcohol readily available, anything was for sale. On most Saturdays there were auction sales in Pavement, as described by William Camidge:

> Not the least interesting was the sale of a woman [in 1839]. She had left her husband through his drunken habits and ill-treatment, and in one of his mad freaks he had brought her into the Market-place ... with a halter round her neck. She was mounted on a table beside the auctioneer, who descanted on her virtues and spoke of her as a clean, industrious, quiet and careful woman, attractive in appearance and well mannered.

The woman went for 7s 6d, halter included, and proceeded to live with her purchaser near to Pavement. Twenty years later her husband died and she married said purchaser; she herself died in the 1880s 'at a great age, respectable and respected'.

Alcohol was a true vote winner. Camidge (1828–1909) gives a graphic account of the near anarchy and corruption that attended elections:

> It was not unusual during the progress of an election to roll into the Pavement large barrels of ale, one end of which was speedily knocked in, and then a scene of indescribable confusion and contention ensued. Men, women and children rushed for the beer barrel, and with every description of kitchen and other utensils they sought to drink their fill, and carry off what unsteady legs, and intense excitement would allow them to get away with. It was no uncommon thing as the beer neared the bottom for someone to fall, or be pushed into the barrel.

Toxic Beer

In 1816 the publicans of York reduced the price of a quart of beer from 6d to 5d (2½d a pint). Great news. However, the brewers then forced their tenants to raise the price again – bad news. When the *York Courant* urged drinkers to boycott beer, the brewers then had second thoughts and reduced the price to a level *below* the original: a thirty-six gallon barrel would now cost 18s less, enabling landlords to sell at a rock bottom 2d per pint. Excellent news, which was spoilt when a letter to the paper by an anonymous Dr... warned of a mysterious epidemic that was killing people off in places like Kirbymoorside. Lead poisoning from beer pumps was said to be the cause as seen in patients 'accustomed to take malt bitter early in the morning'.

On another note, the *Courant* recommended a solution to beer of poor quality: simply add a large spoonful of mustard powder to a jug of 14 gallons of beer. Within 24 hours the beer will be thin and clear, and it will taste good.

And, on a much more sober note:

The Poor Clare Colettines

The forty Poor Clare Colettines nuns came to York from Bruges. The first convent of the Sisters of the Second Order of Saint Francis was Plantation House in Hull Road in 1865; they moved to the obscure St Joseph's Monastery in Lawrence Street in 1873 (recently demolished). Until recently they lived there behind twenty-feet high walls, got up at 5.00 a.m., lived in silence, were vegetarians and cultivated a six-acre garden to make themselves largely self-sufficient. As the photograph shows, the time-honoured monastic practice of beer and wine production was high on the agenda.

Self-sufficiency in wine.

At its height during the 1940s, the convent was home to more than forty nuns. The convent comprised cloisters, cells, chapel and a refectory. The remaining eight Poor Clare Colettines have now moved to Askham Bryan. The convent's Mother Abbess sought permission from the Vatican for the move and admitted to mixed feelings: 'it's only bricks and mortar' she said.

IS IT THE SPIRITS, OR
IS IT A ... GHOST?

Waiting for a ghost.

Ghosts, it seems, are everywhere and York has more than its fair share, with 500 or so phantoms to its name. Many of them, it would appear, have a predilection for York's pubs ... so York pubs feature prominently in the roll call of spirits. Here is a short ghost tour of the York (mainly) pub ghost scene.

There is the girl at 5 College Street who starved to death after her parents died from plague; and in Bedern where a number of orphans died at the nearby Industrial Ragged School during the 1800s, due to the negligence of the alcoholic schoolmaster, some people walking by the arch have been taken by the hand by a small child, accompanied by giggling and screaming ... at St Williams' College the ghosts of two 16th century brothers appear – they murdered a priest here: one betrayed the other; the one hanged, the other went mad.

Elsewhere you can be terrified by ... the ghost of the philandering, flashing Duke of Buckingham in the Cock and Bottle on Skeldergate – only ever seen by women – he showed up once while the landlady was in the shower (*Psycho*ghost?); the ghost that attends every funeral in All Saint's church in Pavement; the Grey Lady who had an affair with a York noble – she was a nun who was bricked up in a wall where the Theatre Royal now stands; the decapitated (or incapacitated) Earl of Northumberland's ghost wanders around Goodramgate looking for his head (some hangover) – he was executed here in 1572 for treason; Lady Alice Peckett, amongst others, haunts the Golden Fleece; Green Jenny ghosts around what was the Five Lions; a group of Roman legionaries march through the walls of the Treasurer's House; Mad Alice hovers around the eponymous lane after her hanging in 1825 for ... just being mad Alice; Catherine Howard, fourth wife of Henry VIII, haunts the King's Manor after her execution soon after staying there.

The York Arms is haunted by another of York's grey ladies, said by some to be a nun. Former landlords and their families – mostly the men – have seen a floating grey mist, floating bellows and other small objects, locked doors opened and open doors shut. Overdoing the stock sampling? The gents' toilets are a favourite haunt where that famous grey mist is often seen.

The Punch Bowl in Stonegate scares us with more than one ghost story. The first tells of a former landlord who was incinerated in a fire; his spirit still walks down the cellar steps, even though the steps have since been removed. On reaching the bottom (of the invisible steps) he disappears into the floor. The pub also has its grey lady, a woman who committed suicide after her lover was unfaithful to her; she keeps coming back looking for her lover. The third ghost is another young woman: one story has it that she was strangled by a drunk in the pub (which was then a brothel in the 18th century) after she rejected his advances. She still runs from room to room trying to get away from him. The other version is that she was a barmaid beaten to death in the 16th century, again frantically trying to evade her murderer in the pub, which wasn't built then.

In Ye Olde Starre Inne a Royalist officer haunts the pub, dating from 1644 when it was a field hospital in the English Civil War. He sports a beaver hat, breeches and doublet, and stands to attention. He shares his 'billet' with two black cats. The cats antagonise any dogs in the pub even today; their bodies are buried in the large pillar in the bar. Finally, there have been occasional reports of an old lady climbing the stairs, seen only by children. This is what is meant by a dog-friendly and children-friendly pub.

In the Yorkshire Terrier pub a girl haunts the cellar; she is reputedly the daughter of a prostitute from the Punch Bowl across Stonegate. It was around here that Laurence Sterne, author of the novel *Tristam Shandy*, stayed. The locals told him why he could hear banging in the house next door, every night just after midnight. Apparently, a previous occupant lived in fear of robbers so every night, after the tolling of the Minster bells at midnight, he frightened off any robbers by repeatedly banging his walking stick on the wall near his bed. The banging continues to this day. Perhaps they were just having noisy sex?

At Thomas's Hotel the chairs and tables in the top floor function room have been seen moving about on their own, and ghostly figures wander up and down the staircases. Reports of hauntings have increased since a pair of ballet shoes that used to be in a glass case on the wall mysteriously went missing.

So haunted is the Black Swan in Peasholme Green that the website can confidently boast that 'A high-impact, rare, or hard-to-predict event far beyond the realm of normal expectations can be referred to as a "Black Swan Event"'. At the time of writing we can identify at least seven poltergeists:

One is a ghost of the gentleman in a bowler hat who appears to be impatiently waiting for someone at the bar – eventually his apparition slowly fades away … another ghost in a long white dress sits staring into the fire in the bar – it is the ghost of a beautiful, glowing flaxen-haired young woman, a jilted bride, and any man staring into her face will die in ecstasy. A small boy, known as Matthew can be seen in the bar and passageway dressed in Victorian clothes; Matthew was a pickpocket, which might explain the routine disappearance of various items kept behind the bar. Jack the highwayman regularly turns up in the kitchen (built over the original stable yard); he is dressed in riding boots and a long black cloak. Jack can be heard singing along to Irish folk songs in the corner of the bar late at night. Whiskey in the Jar? A ghostly large black cat wanders around the pub, and should anyone have the temerity to sit in the chair by the fire they will be cursed. Finally, in a definitive definition of 'legless', a pair of legs can be seen (or not) disappearing up the stairs.

Here's Jack the Highwayman in the 70s, or is it just Dick Turpin?

Be scared.

THE LOST PUBS OF YORK

York, like everywhere in the land, has seen many pubs come and go. Pubs, and their names, be they the names of pubs still open or now closed, are equally vocal about the past. Indeed, the history and culture of a town or city can, up to a point, be read through a description of the pubs that remain open or which have closed. York is a good example of this.

The footprint that a pub leaves behind reveals so much about local business and industry, about local sport and leisure, about (in)famous local men and women and about key historical events.

Here are just some of the unfortunate casualties. What is obvious from a short glance at this list is the frequency with which pubs change their names – at the drop of a beer mat – to reflect changing demographics and fashions, or to commemorate historical events. Often, to add to the confusion, they later revert to their original names. Equally noticeable, as mentioned above, is what York pub names tell us about local, history, business and industry, be it railways, glass, printing or brewing. Chocolate- and Rowntree-related pub vocabulary, though, is notably absent and may be accounted for by the Rowntree family's temperance principles – were it not for non Quaker Joseph Terry …

RIP the following:

18 Cert, Gillygate – previously the Bay Horse.

Adelphi, Micklegate – Corruption notwithstanding, George Hudson did York the favour of establishing the city as a major railway centre. His lasting legacy was the formation of the North Eastern Railway company in 1854, headed by Hudson's enemy George Leeman; York to London could now be covered in five hours. Ethical, transparent and principled Hudson was not, but he was visionary and made an invaluable and unrivalled contribution to the railways and the economy of the United Kingdom; York was a major beneficiary and continues to benefit to this day. In 1849, in a lame attempt to erase him from local history, George Hudson Street in York was renamed Railway Street; in 1971 the street was renamed again after the Railway King who had presciently brought the railways to York.

Plaques decorate the walls of former homes at 44 Monkgate and 1 College Street. The old twenty-three-bedroom 1851 Adelphi temperance pub on the corner of Micklegate took the name The Railway King in 1880, and, presumably at the same time, arranged for a licence to sell alcohol. His name also lives on at Hudson House, formerly the 1968 offices for the northeastern region of British Rail. The Adelphi was built on the site of a pub called the Royal Oak, later the Ship from 1647. Edwards and Reflex are modern, anodyne, names for the place.

Admiral Hawke, Walmgate – This pub opened in 1795 and named after 1st Lord Hawke (1705–1781) who defeated the French at Quiberon Bay in 1759. There was a dram shop; the pub closed in 1951. It was also known as the Lord Hawke, and, erroneously, the Admiral Oak in 1825.

Albert Inn, George Street – A 12-feet-wide beerhouse on the corner of Albert Street (hence the name). Family and customers shared the toilet via the family kitchen. It closed in 1903 and was bought by the York & Equitable Society who converted it into a shop.

Albion, Goodramgate – A 1857 beerhouse next to the Albion Iron and Brass factory just inside Monk Bar. Sold 1859.

Albion, Parliament Street – Once the Yorkshireman until 1841. In 1877 it sported its own brewery. It closed in 1881.

Albion, St Andrewgate – Before this it was the Brewer's Arms, near as it was to Hunt's brewery. It was also the Angler's Arms in 1867 (see Snickleway Arms) and closed in 1872.

Alexandra, Market Street – Horse & Jockey and Turf Tavern were previous names up to 1876. The pub was named after Princess Alexandra, wife of Albert Edward, Prince of Wales. There were four rooms for travellers; there was also a concert room and dram shop on the first floor with a kitchen on second floor. It closed in 1937

Alice Hawthorn, Wheldrake – See the Nun Monkton entry for the pub of the same name for the equine derivation of the name – by Muley-Moloch out of Rebecca. However, Alice Hawthorn was also the *nom de plume* of Septimus Winner (1827–1902), the American songwriter famous for *Maryland, My Maryland*. It closed in 1999.

(Evelyn Collection, courtesy of Yorkshire Architectural and York Archaeological Society)

Alma Tavern, Alma Terrace – Opened in 1872. It was named after the Alma River in Crimea and the battle fought there.

Anchor, First Water Lane (King's Staith) – It was up for sale in 1766; it was known as Crown & Anchor after 1841.

Anchor, Queen's Staith – The Queen's Staith Inn before that, from 1855. The dram shop was little used on account of flooding. A family shared the toilet with drinkers. It closed in 1905. The Methodists bought it to use as a Men's Institute and a caretaker's house for the Skeldergate Mission.

The building plastered with posters, around 1920. (Evelyn Collection, courtesy of Yorkshire Architectural and York Archaeological Society)

Arrows, Gillygate – Also known as the Sign of the Arrows.

Artichoke, Micklegate – First and last records were in 1783 and 1829. In 1795 it was the punning Harty Chalk and later the Barefoot.

Bar Hotel, Micklegate – The building, near the bar, was originally a barber's until 1867 when it became a pub. From 1996 it rejoiced in the silly name Scruffy Murphy's and then later the mercifully plain the Micklegate. Next door but one was the Barefoot (closed 1928), while over the road was the Jolly Bacchus – demolished in 1873 for street widening.

The site of the Bar Hotel is under the building on the left. (Evelyn Collection, courtesy of Yorkshire Architectural and York Archaeological Society)

153

Some say that the Artichoke and the Barefoot were one and the same. Barefoot was a chestnut colt by Tramp out of Rosamund, which won the 1823 St Leger.

Barefoot, Micklegate; or Horse Barefoot – It was a beerhouse in 1862 with full licence by 1902. See above. It closed in 1927.

Barge, River Ouse at Terry Avenue – This was a former grain barge converted to a pub and night club in 1979. It sank in 1984; it was refloated and towed to Naburn Lock in 1985 where it was 'scuttled'. The Flying Dutchman took over.

Barleycorn: Coppergate, Davygate, Walmgate and Bedern – The Coppergate pub was once the Blue Bell until 1801; Davygate was the Wheatsheaf. Walmgate is first recorded in 1795, changing to the Hope & Anchor by 1830 and later the Full Moon.

Barley Sheaf, Nunnery Lane – This was a beerhouse. Once the Golden Ball, then the Wheatsheaf between 1840 and 1848; it was the Crown and then the Wheatsheaf again.

Barrack Tavern, Fulford Road – Named after the nearby cavalry barracks in 1801. It nearly became part of the artillery barracks in 1880. It was known as the Fulford Arms in 1976.

Barrack Tavern, Lowther Street – It was the Blacksmith's Arms until 1852. It took on the military name because it was close to the Militia Stores Depot.

Barrel Inn, Little Blake Street – This was possibly the same pub as the Shakespeare Tavern, named for its proximity to the theatre.

Barstow Arms, Askham Bryan – Named after the Barstow family who lived in the village and built two almshouses there in 1862. It was later the Nag's Head.

Bay Horse, Aldwark – It was first heard of in 1822 but before that it may have been the Leopard and the Spotted Dog.

Bay Horse, Elvington – Opened in 1823; the name was changed to Grey Horse in 1840.

Bay Horse, Gillygate – Recorded from 1822. Much later it was the 18 Cert.

Bay Horse, Goodramgate – Opened in 1818; Square & Compasses (1849); Joiners' Arms (1851).

Bay Horse, Hungate – Opened in 1858. It was also known as the Cotherstone.

Hungate derives from Hundgate – street of the dogs – a common Viking street name. As a result of Seebohm Rowntree's *Poverty,* in 1908 and 1914 York's medical officer, Edmund Smith, produced reports condemning streets in Hungate and Walmgate as unfit for habitation:

> The back yards in Hope Street and Albert Street and in some other quarters can only be viewed with repulsion – they are so small and fetid, and so hemmed-in by surrounding houses and other buildings… There are no amenities; it is an absolute slum.

At the 1921 census York's population was 84,052 with 18,608 inhabited houses (= 4.5 persons per dwelling).

Bay Horse, Mint Yard – It was once called the Horse & Groom.

Bay Horse, Murton – It was formerly the Jerry and the Horse & Jockey.

Bay Horse, Walmgate – Opened in 1753. Also the White Horse (1823) and the Spotted Dog (1876). Family and customers shared the only WC. It was closed by 1970.

Baynes' Coffee house, Petergate – The Ancient Society of York Florists met here in 1804. William Baynes became a freeman of York in 1798 and took the posts of macebearer in 1800 and swordbearer in 1813. It was renamed Baynes' Hotel in 1813, reverting to its former name in 1828. The Ancient Society of York Florists was established in 1768; it is the world's oldest horticultural society and runs the world's longest-running flower show; it is now at Askham Bryan but before that was in Colliergate and at Baynes' Coffee House.

Bear, Coney Street – It was first mentioned in 1573 on the site of the Golden Lion. The George & Dragon was here later, later the George.

Bear, Fossgate – First mentioned in 1753.

Bear's Paw, Micklegate – Up for sale in 1891.

Bedroom, Micklegate – Opened in 2002. Previously, it was Harry's Bar.

Beech Tree, Goodramgate – 1848–1872. Previous names were the Fox and the Lord Byron.

Beehive, Peter Lane – Replaced the Three Tuns here. Beerhouse here in 1863. The landlord was fined for keeping eighteen prostitutes here in 1870.

Bell, Micklegate – Once the Blue Bell. The licence was transferred to the Imperial in Crichton Avenue in 1937.

Beverley Arms, High Petergate – Leased from the Dean and Chapter from 1799. It closed in 1848.

Billiard Table, Stonegate – Noted in 1731 as the Sign of the Billiard Table. Also known as Keregan's.

Bird in Hand, Bootham – Demolished to make way for Exhibition Square when the bar barbican was torn down in 1835. It was rebuilt next to Queen Margaret's Arch and was known as St Leonard's Hotel for a while before moving again into Bootham as the Exhibition.

Bishop Blase, Coppergate – Named after the unfortunate Bishop Blase in 1770. The Bishop of Sebaste in Armenia was martyred in 316 ce when he was painfully and comprehensively lacerated with wool combs before his decapitation. Some post mortem consolation came with his canonisation at the Council of Lyons in 1244 and his institution as the patron saint of wool working. His feast day is 3 February, important in York in the late 15th century. It is also the day from 1737 when the new city chamberlains took office each year.

Black Bull, St Sampson's Square
(Courtesy and © of York Press)

Black Bull, Bootham – It belonged to the Merchant Adventurers approximately from 1495 until 1564. A Merchant Adventurer was a merchant who risked his own money in pursuit of his trade or craft. For centuries, up until 1835 when the Municipal Corporations Act transferred control to local councils, the Guilds were all-powerful and controlled York's trade and industry. To do business in the city it was necessary to be elected a Freeman of the City: a man or a woman had to be a Freeman before membership was allowed to the craft guilds. The Merchant Adventurers' Guild goes back to 1357 when a number of prominent York men and women joined together to form a religious fraternity and to build the Merchant Adventurers' Hall in Fossgate. By 1430 most members were merchants of one kind or another; they then set up a trading association or guild using the Great Hall to conduct their business affairs and to meet socially, to look after the poor in the almshouses in the Undercroft and to worship in the Chapel.

Black Bull, Davygate – First recorded in 1770; later the Little Black Bull.

Black Bull, Hull Road – First recorded in 1840; rebuilt as a road house in 1935.

Black Bull, Osbaldwick – First recorded in 1823. It was known as The Derwent Arms from 1937.

Black Bull, St Sampson's Square.

The Turkish Baths in St Sampson's Square later became Shepherd's City Baths and continued to offer Turkish and slipper baths. They were flanked by pubs: the Golden Lion on the left (run by M. Bullivant and serving John J. Hunt's ales); the Black Bull Hotel, also on the left; and the Three Cranes and the Exchange across the square, the latter an H. Bentley & Co. house. Rhodes Brown, haberdashers, was next to the Three Cranes. The first mention of the Black Bull comes in a bull-baiting advertisement in 1687 and as a rendezvous for curriers. A jettied building, it had a brewery in 1858 as well as a singing room and a dressing room for the singers. Customers and a family shared the single WC; the urinal in the yard was embarrassingly visible from overlooking cottages. In 1903 it expanded into the Hand and Heart next door.

(Evelyn Collection, courtesy of Yorkshire Architectural and York Archaeological Society)

A slave market is said to have existed in St Sampson's Square during the Roman occupation. Later, Bede tells us that Pope Gregory I (d. 604 ce) admired English slaves, punning *'non Anglised angeli'* – 'they're not Angles, but angels'. More recently, in 1909 the use of slave labour on cocoa plantations became a controversial and embarrassing ethical issue for the chocolate industry, particularly Fry, Cadbury and Rowntree, philanthropists and Quakers all. Despite legislation, the use of what was effectively state-sanctioned slave labour continued in West Africa – a major source of raw materials for the chocolate makers; the outcome of reports from the Quaker Joseph Buritt and Henry Nevison for *Harper's Weekly* was that all three companies would boycott cocoa from Portuguese colonial San Thome and Principe.

(Evelyn Collection, courtesy of Yorkshire Architectural and York Archaeological Society)

St Sampson, after whom the square is named, is the only church in the country dedicated to St Sampson. According to Geoffrey of Monmouth's *History of the Kings of Britain*, he was installed by King Arthur's uncle, Ambrosius Aurelianus, as Archbishop of York after repelling a force of Saxon invaders in ad 466. This Sampson, of course, has nothing to do with the Samson in the Bible – he of the long hair and Delilah.

Black Bull, Walmgate – Up for sale in 1809. The family and customers shared the WC, which also saw service as a urinal. The 1906 Brewster Sessions declared it one of the six worst houses in York and rescinded its licence.

Black Dog – There were Black Dogs in High Ousegate (1770), Coppergate (sold 1765), St Saviourgate (1849), Thursday Market (sold 1810), Feasegate (1783–1828),

Jubbergate (1787), 5 Low Jubbergate (1818) and known from 1830 as the Original Back Dog and the Dog from 1846.

Black Dog, 59 Low Jubbergate – It is not to be confused with the Black Dog at No. 5; it was known as the Old Black Dog from 1822–1834.

Black Horse – Black Horses were in profusion too. Black Horse Passage, Fossgate (Tenter's Passage) – a den of thieves and whores (1783); Blake Street, sold to the owners of the Assembly Rooms in 1734 and demolished; Bootham (1745) had a brew house in 1851 and was rebuilt in 1867 reopening as the Bootham Tavern; Hosier Street (Pavement, 1743-1861); Walmgate (1733) – the WC for customers and the family was in the cellar.

The Bootham Black Horse can be seen on the left in the middle of the street line. (Evelyn Collection, courtesy of Yorkshire Architectural and York Archaeological Society)

Black Lion, Jubbergate – 1752. On the corner of Feasegate. Hosted a canary show in 1784.

Blackmoor's Head, Colliergate – 1770. Also on Low Petergate on the corner with Stonegate (1755).

Blacksmith's Arms are plentiful, largely because the village blacksmith doubled as a publican: Acomb (sold 1819); Ackham Richard (1876); Church Street (1818) changed to the Harcourt Arms by 1851 and included a brewhouse, later the Talbot (a now extinct breed of large hunting dogs); Dunnington – known too as the Smith's Arms – 1872–1876 was the Horseshoe, closed in 1909; over Foss Bridge (1806): Lowther Street (1852), also the Barrack Tavern; Main Street, Fulford also known as

the Saddle in 1815, now the White Horse on the opposite side of the road; Naburn; Osbaldwick, also called the Horseshoe; Rufforth, previously the Buck, closed in 1999; Skelton (1823); Wheldrake was renamed the Wenlock Arms in 1856. The Blacksmith's Arms at Flaxton was an 18th century coaching inn, and is now a B&B; it is pictured here in the early 1900s.

158

Black Swans, too, were in profusion: Askham Richard (1823), also the Swan; Bishopthorpe (1838), preceded the Woodman?; Ouse Bridge (1741); Low Petergate (1841), once the Bricklayers' Arms and the Eclipse.

Black Swan, Coney Street. Opposite the George, under what was British Home Stores is the Black Swan, a medieval building, rebuilt in 1790, to follow the new building line of Coney Street. The Black Swan was one of York's major coaching inns.

(Courtesy and © of York Press)

In 1706 on 12 April, the first stagecoach from London to York left the Black Swan, Holborn, for York's Black Swan, at 5 a.m. It took four days. In 1786, mail coaches first appeared, and by 1830 eighteen coaches daily left the Black Swan. In 1838 the time from London to York was down to twenty-one hours. There was stabling for 100 horses here.

Stagecoaches included:

'Express' to Carlisle – W, F am
'Tally Ho' to Carlisle – T, Th, S
'Rockingham' to Hull – every forenoon
'Trafalgar' to Hull – every afternoon
'Union' to Kendal – every morning
'True Blue' to Leeds – every afternoon

Many celebrities stayed here including Dickens and the Bronte Sisters.

The Royal Agricultural Society was inaugurated in 1837 by a group of agriculturalists at a meeting in the Black Swan Hotel, Coney Street. They decided that their objectives would be to establish 'an annual meeting for the exhibition of farming stock, implements, etc. and for the general promotion of agriculture'. The sign now resides in the Castle Museum.

Black Swan, Front Street, Acomb – 1814. Also the Swan. The pub hosted the coroner's enquiry here after the Acomb Landing tragedy when the sons and daughters of John and Ann Rigg went for a boating trip on the Ouse on 19 August 1830, with friends. Their rowing boat collided with a keel near Acomb landing, and they were thrown into the water. Six members of the family were drowned. Public grief was so great that it prompted a subscription fund to pay for what was once a grand memorial, with a marble sculpture by William Plows, and a specially commissioned poem from Sheffield poet James Montgomery. Sadly, the memorial is dilapidated today. The good news is that the undergrowth has been removed recently and the Civic Trust is actively exploring ways to restore the monument.

The inscription once read:

RAISED BY FRIENDSHIP IN MEMORY OF FOUR SONS AND TWO
DAUGHTERS OF JOHN AND ANN RIGG, OF THIS CITY;

VIZ. ANN GUTHRIE RIGG, AGED 19 YEARS; ELIZA RIGG, AGED 17;
THOMAS GORWOOD RIGG, AGED 18; JOHN RIGG, AGED 16; JAMES
SMITH RIGG, AGED 7; AND CHARLES RIGG, AGED 6

WHO WERE DROWNED BY THEIR BOAT BEING RUN DOWN ON
THE RIVER OUSE, NEAR York, AUGUST 19, 1830.

Bloomsbury, Grape Lane – 1841. Named after a bay colt out of Arcot Lass, 1839 Derby winner; called the Fying Dutchman by 1855.

Blue Anchor, First Water Lane – 1787. Also Low Ousegate (1767).

Blue Ball, Holgate – 1754. Opposite the Fox. It was demolished in 1823. It was sometimes called the Blue Bell and First Water Lane (1781).

Blue Bell, Fossgate – 1769. On the corner with Hosier Street (Pavement). Not to be confused with the Blue Bell on Fossgate, which, thankfully, survives today. Other Blue Bells were in Bootham (1761); Coppergate (1782), Barleycorn by 1801; Feasegate (1751); Micklegate (1795); North Street (1839); Skeldergate, let 1781, opposite the Old Crane; St Mary, Castlegate parish (1783); St Sampson's Square (1750); Walmgate (1795), closed in 1958.

Blue Boar, Goodramgate – Two pubs in Goodramgate glory in this name. One (1772) became the Royal Oak and the Blue Pig; the other is from 1795. There was a Blue Boar in Thursday Market from 1773.

Bluitt's Inn, Museum Street – Formerly Gibson's, then Ringrose's (1785), then Etridge's Royal Hotel (1803).

Boar, Blossom Street – On the corner of Holgate Road. Castlegate: in 1485 Sir Roger Cotam met here in fear of his life 'at the sign of the boore' to proclaim Henry VII king in succession to Richard III, slain at Bosworth.

Boards were everywhere: Bishophill Senior (1858); Bridge Street (1822) but known as Rooke's Dram Shop in 1823, the new Bridge Street Hotel and Ye Olde No. 5, 5 being the street number; Coppergate (1822), also called the Three Tuns; Fossgate – also known as Seller's Vaults and Seller's Dram Shop with its beer bottling business and no conveniences, it was demolished in 1957 to make way for Stonebow; two in Goodramgate: one that became the Snickleway Arms, the other opened in 1895 as a shop for W.H. Thackwray who took over John March's brewery behind it in Ogleforth in 1880 and also went by the name of Thackwray's; High Ousegate (1830); 94 High Petergate (= York Arms); 106 High Petergate was initially Wolstenholme's Dram Shop in 1869, Haigh's Vaults in 1887 and Petergate Wine and Spirit Stores and Bar in 1902 (now the Hole in the Wall); Jubbergate 1823; 5 Low Ousegate, wine and spirits merchants (1823); 9 Low Ousegate, a beerhouse also known as McGregor's House; 16 Low Ousegate (1838) with its bottling room and stores also named Hillyard's Wine Lodge, the Lodge, Yates' Wine Lodge, Dukes of York and O'Neills; Low Petergate preceded Gibson's Vaults; Marygate (1823); Micklegate (1872) wine and spirit merchants became Walker's in 1973; Middlethorpe (1823) later the Horse and the Horseshoe; North Street, a beerhouse in 1834; Spurriergate (1872) – the shop for Brett Brother's City Brewery established in 1858 in Church Lane next to the Greyhound. J.J. Hunt bought it in 1897 – it closed in 1958 along with the Greyhound.

Bonding Warehouse, Skeldergate; a conversion from a warehouse built in 1873 and once used by Rowntrees. It opened in 1981. Flooding closed it in 2000.

Boot & Shoe, Dunnington – 1857. A beerhouse, closed between 1909 and 1921; Upper Poppleton, once the Brickmakers' Arms on the A59; Walmgate (1783).

Boot & Slipper, Bedern – 1818. Bedern was not the place to be wandering around after dark; the pub must have presented some additional challenges. It was an unsavoury, violent and impoverished place at the best of times with 300 people sharing just five toilets according to one report. On 10 October 1868 *The Yorkshire Gazette* reported on what was probably a typical day in Bedern with this encounter between John Rohan, Patrick Muldowney, Michael McMennamy and Bridget Rohan:

> Complainant [McMennamy] went out of his own house … when John Rohan went behind him and struck him on the head with a poker … two girls were fighting at the same time … and notwithstanding the blow he tried to separate them and then Muldowney struck him with half a brick … and while prostrate Bridget went out with a rolling pin and gave him some rattlers on the head, and the others kicked him … John Rohan and Molly Rohan were also charged with assaulting Thomas McMennamy, son of the above-named complainant … the girl struck him with an iron bolt and also bit his finger.

Bowling Green, Groves Lane – 1818. There is still a bowling green nearby but not the pub.

Boy & Barrel, Bar Lane – A popular interpretation of the image on the sign of the Jolly Bacchus: an obese child perched on a barrel.

Bradford Arms, St Sampson's Square – Other names are the Greyhound, Reindeer, Stag. This was one of Hotham's & Co's fifty-four houses, all later sold to Tadcaster Tower Brewery in 1882.

Brewers Arms, Tanner Row – 1843. Had a beer shop with 'pint pot trade' and cottage attached to it; St Andrewgate – 1841. Earlier names were the Anglesey Arms and the **Albion**; **Walmgate** (1841) – one of York's six worst houses according to the Chief Constable in 1906.

Bricklayers' Arms, Palmer Lane – 1838. Famous for its linnet singing contests; Peasholme Green (up for sale 1852); Peter Lane (1809); Low Petergate – the Black

Swan by 1841; Walmgate (1851–1861), previously known as the Malt Shovel and the Old Malt Shovel, then the Spread Eagle; Upper Poppleton, which was the Boot & Shoe in 1857.

Bridge Hotel, Huntington Road – At Bell Farm; by 1993 it was the Fossway, named after the river nearby.

Bridge Inn, Layerthorpe – 1867. Had a dram shop, family and customers shared the WC.

(Courtesy and © of York Press)

Briefing Room, St Helen's Square – On 1 February 1945 J.E. Mcdonald was the first of 600 airmen to scratch their names on the mirror at Betty's during World War II. Also known as Betty's Bar or the Dive, it was a regular haunt of the hundreds of airmen stationed in and around York; these included many Canadians from No. 6 Bomber Group. One signatory, Jim Rogers, borrowed a waitress's diamond ring to scratch his name on the mirror.

Briggs' Coffee House, Stonegate – 1798–1799. Renamed the Saracen's Head Coffee House (1809) and then the Saracen's Head.

Britannia, Acomb; Heworth – 1806. When it closed in 1967 the licence went to the Walnut Tree opposite; Nunnery Lane (1837); Walmgate (1818): first known as the Britannia Coffee House.

British Tar, North Street – 1843. Also known as the Fortunate Tar.

Brown Cow, Minster Gates – 1770. Paragon Street (1770); Petergate (1767); St Lawrence parish (1787).

Bull (later the Rose) – Coney Street was owned by the Mayor and Corporation. In 1459 in the reign of Henry VI it was

> ordained that from this day forth, no aliens coming from foreign parts, shall be lodged within the said city, liberties or suburbs thereof, but only in the Inn of the Mayor and Commonalty, at the sign of the Bull in Conying Street.

One of the first records of any inn in the city of York and an early form of nationalisation at a local level. In 1497 we know that Frederick Freez, a 'bookebynder and Stacyoner', rented land adjacent to the Rose (the Bull). We learn from Robert Davies (1793–1875) in his *Antiquarian Walks through York* that there was an inn in Lopp Lane (where the top of Blake Street is today) showing the sign of the Dragon. In 1484 John Tynley was playing dice here when he went outside to urinate, having left a piece of gold on the board; on his return the gold had gone, at which he filed a complaint with the Lord Mayor.

Brunswick, Fishergate – 1902. A beerhouse, also known as the Fishergate Tavern. Family and customers made do with a privy in the back yard; Parliament Street (1851), then the Brunswick Vaults in 1855 with its own brewing plant.

Buck, Minster Close – Once called the Horse & Groom; North Street (1795); Rufforth (1823); St John del Pike parish (1783).

Bumper Castle, Wigginton Road – The Bumper Castle was built by William Johnson, landlord of The Three Cranes in York until 1846. His widow took over on his death in 1879. She was the oldest licensee in the UK when she died aged 102 in 1907. Rebuilt soon after, it is now a restaurant, the Brew & Brisket.

Burland's Coffee House, Micklegate – 1824. Formerly the Crown, the Grapes and the Golden Cup, the Cup and Burland's Hotel; Tanner Row – next door to the Great Northern.

Burns' Hotel, Lawrence Street – Once the St Nicholas, and the Tam O'Shanter (1854).

Butchers' Arms, Shambles – A wholly apt name for a pub in this the street of butchers. There were three other pubs here: The Globe (closed 1936); The Eagle and Child (closed 1925); and The Shoulder of Mutton (closed 1898). The Butchers' Arms/Neptune closed 1903.

Castle Howard Ox, Nessgate. Also the Fat Ox?

Cattle Market Inn, Fawcett Street – Serving the farmers at the market. Once the Paragon Inn. Shared WC between family and customers; renovated in 1980 only to close in 1983.

Cattle Market Inn, St Dennis Street – 1843?

Cattle Market Tavern, Heslington Road – 1858.

The so aptly named Shoulder of Mutton is on the left.

City Arms, Fawcett Street – Opened in 1829, when the cattle market was built. Also known as the New Market Hotel. At one time used as a social club for sportsmen.

City Arms, 174 Walmgate – 1843. The WC was shared with the shop next door.

Clarence Hotel, Davygate. – 1851. Also Addison's Hotel then St Helen's Hotel.

Clifford's Tower, Peasholme Green, Haymarket after 1827 – Opened in 1783. Also the Tower, then The Leeds Arms from 1827.

Clock Inn, Parliament Street
(Courtesy and © of York Press)

Clock Inn, Parliament Street – 1867. Once the Eagle and the Clock & Eagle. Walmgate, 1845: + brewhouse and dramshop; family WC shared with customers.

Coach and Horses, Jubbergate – The sign depicted the coach and horses but the writing made no such reference, saying instead Saynors after the family which ran it. The Coach and Horses in Nessgate was known as Big Coach; that in Micklegate as Little Coach (now the Priory).

Coach & Horses, Low Ousegate – Once Harrison's Coffee House (1812) and the Commercial Coffee House (1824). Ellis's Hotel, 1841. It was demolished in 1904 to allow Nessgate to be widened and a new pub with the same name was erected in Low Ousegate/King Street.

There were other Coach & Horses at King Street, 1879; Kexby Bridge, 1823; Little Stonegate, 1828; Micklegate, 1818; Mint Yard, 1770; Newgate, 1838; Walmgate, 1749.

Coachmakers' Arms, Little Stonegate – 1818.

Cooper – The Barrell Churn and the Barrell in the late 18th century and the Mail Coach after that for 140 years; now the Roman Bath.

Coffee House, Davygate – 1824; also in Lendal, 1812; Micklegate, 1824; Nessgate, 1795; Stonegate, 1783 = Brigg's Coffee House?

Commercial Hotel, Tanner Row – This was a temperance hotel in 1893. The laying of tram lines between Railway Street and Rougier Street did for it in 1908.

Compass, Middle Water Lane – 1822. It became the Square & Compass.

Corner House, Burton Stone Lane – 1837.

Cotherstone, Hungate – 1846. It was on the corner of Carmelite Street. It was named after a bay colt. Previously, it was the Whale Fishery.

Cowper, Micklegate – 1569 – recorded as a place where the Corpus Christi plays were to be performed.

Craven Ox Head, George Street – 1840 changed to the Newcastle Arms in 1867.

Cressland, Micklegate – 1550.

Cricketers Arms, Tanner Row – 1846. Named by Richard Letby, a celebrated cricketer and captain of York Cricket Club. Also, Davygate – formerly the Cricketers' Resort (1865); Turf Coffee House and then the London Hotel after a rebuild; Gillygate, formerly the Three Arrows and the Earl of Dublin, a title of Albert Edward, Prince of Wales.

Cricket Ground, Trinity Lane – 1834. Formerly the Square & Compass, the Cup, and Compass' then the Seven Stars and the Half Moon.

Cross Guns, Minster Yard – 1742.

Crown Hotel, Micklegate.

Crow's Coffee House, Coney Street – Also known as the White Horse.

Crystal Palace, Swinegate; once the Lord Nelson.

Cutt-a-Feather, St Sampson's Square – Became the Nagg's Head in 1711; later it was the White Horse Inn.

(Evelyn Collection, courtesy of Yorkshire Architectural and York Archaeological Society)

Cygnet – On the corner of Price Street and Cygnet Street.

Dray, Harmarket – 1818.

Duke's Head Coffee House, Bridge Street.

Eagle & Child, Pavement – 1537. Robert Aske's body was taken here after decapitation. Aske was one of the leaders of the Pilgrimage of Grace who was hanged in chains from Clifford's Tower for his troubles by Henry VIII in 1537. He died a slow death a week later; his body was left there for a year as a putrefying warning to other potential traitors.

YORK. THE SHAMBLES.

Eagle & Child, Shambles – Once named the Reuben's Head. Now there is an Eagle & Child in High Petergate.

Ebor Vaults, Church Street – 1861.

Eden Berys, Goodramgate – 1483.

Edward VII, Nunnery Lane – 1905. First it was a beerhouse named Wright's House.

Elephant and Castle, Skeldergate – 1730. Peasholme Green in1639.

Elephant & Falcon, Stonegate – Once, it was the Old Post House.

Engine Drivers' Rest, Mount Ephraim – 1846. 'A four-roomed cottage'. It was doomed when NER moved the carriage works to Darlington in 1905.

Enterprise Club – Peasholme Green and Walmgate York had not escaped the craze for skiffle: in 1958 the Columba Club in Sir Thomas Herbert's House was Friday night host to the Planets, comprising one thirteen-year-old and four fourteen-year-olds, all from St Michael's College in Leeds. Youth clubs closed at 9.30 p.m. and at weekends and there was nothing much in the dance halls for younger people, until, that is, Father John Murphy opened his beat club in his Our Lady's church in Acomb in 1963. Neil Guppy was the trendsetter, though, when from 1961 he started the Enterprise Club and put on jive parties at Clifton Cinema Ballroom on Fridays, and at the Woolpack in Peasholme Green on Wednesdays and Saturdays, in Acomb Church Hall and in Betty's Bar. By 1966, twenty-seven-year-old Neil had 1,500 members and gave up his teaching post to concentrate on his evening job. The Enterprise Club was in Dixon's Yard, Walmgate, by 1966.

In September 1964 the York Theatre Royal had made a valiant attempt to get in on the act, booking the Merseybeats and Little Eva; sadly, it came to nothing when the Merseybeats, 'exhausted from the strain of touring', cancelled. That same summer, the *Evening Press* was reporting 'a beat groups boom in York', but more bad luck was to ensue: the much vaunted Attic club in Clifford Street, destined to be run by teenagers, hit financial problems in 1965 before it opened; the Pretty Things were very late for their Zarf Club gig in Stonegate after a crash involving the van carrying their instruments. Local group Gideon's Few stood in for them and loaned them their kit. Gideon's Few it was who played a record-breaking ten-hour marathon set non-stop in the Zarf Club in September 1965.

Etridge's Royal Hotel, a coaching inn, was in Narrow Lop Lane or Little Blake Street accessed through Peter Gate and widened in 1860 and 1864 to create Duncombe Place and a vista of the Minster. The hotel boasted a gentleman's club room and a newsroom, which was 'well supplied with the metropolitan and provincial journals'. Etridge's Royal Hotel was demolished in 1859 for the York Poor Law Union.

Fighting Cocks, Walmgate – 1746.

First Hussar, North Street – Previously the Yorkshire Tavern, the Yorkshire Hussar and the Other Tap & Spile.

Fishing Boat, Acaster Malbis – 1822. Later the Fisherman's Arms.

Flying Dutchman, Terry Avenue – Converted from a 130-foot 1940 Dutch motor ship. It replaced the Barge, which sank in 1984. It was named after a phantom ship that was destined to haunt the high seas after a murder was committed on board, ever trying to reach Table Bay, Cape Town. You were doomed if you ever sighted the *Flying Dutchman*. Sightings confirm the ship glowed with ghostly light. If hailed by another ship, the crew of the *Flying Dutchman* will send messages to land, or to people long dead.

Fortunate Tar, North Street – Or the Jolly Sailor.

(Old) Fortune of War, Low Ousegate.

In the 1920s. (Evelyn Collection, courtesy of Yorkshire Architectural and York Archaeological Society)

Fossway (previously the Bridge) – Huntington Road.

Foundry Tavern, George Street.

Fountain, Coney Street – Formerly the Fountain Coffee House.

Four Alls, Stockton-on-the-Forest – 1876. The name derives from the four universal aphorisms: The King (or Queen) rules for all; The Priest prays for all; The Soldier fights for all; The Ordinary Man or farmer pays for all.

Fox, Nether Poppleton – Also the Cross Keys; Goodramgate, once the Beech Tree and the Lord Byron.

Fox & Hounds, Copmanthorpe – 1867.

Free Gardeners' Arms, Townend Street – 1841. It was named after the Order of Ancient Free Gardeners' Lancashire Union – a friendly society for workers founded 1820 to help with medical and funeral costs. It was the Trumpet by 1858 and the Gardeners' Arms in 1846.

Flying Dutchman around 1985.

Freemasons' Arms, Little Blake Street – Originally Freemasons' Arms Coffee House.

Friendly Tavern, Dennis Street – Pre-1869 beerhouse.

Frog Hall Tavern, Layerthorpe – 1828. Possibly named after a racehorse.

Gallows House – Or the White House, Tadcaster Road in 1920. The gloomy name was preceded by the New Inn in 1731. The 17th century building is so named due to its proximity to Tyburn. Later years saw it in use as a laundry and as a dairy (as here); it was demolished in 1955.

(Evelyn Collection, courtesy of Yorkshire Architectural and York Archaeological Society)

Garricks Head, Low Petergate – 1829. Also the Garrick Coffee House, 1829, and named after the famous actor David Garrick.

George, Bootham Bar – 1516.

The George Hotel, Coney Street – One of York's principle coaching inns, serving Hull, Manchester and Newcastle, in Coney Street opposite the Black Swan and the offices of the *York Courant* until 1869 when the inn was tragically knocked down to make way for Leak & Thorp; in 1867 it was called Winn's George Hotel. There was an earlier inn on the site called the Bull but the landlord, Thomas Kaye, Sheriff of York, replaced this with the George in 1614. Sadly, the railways did for the George and it was auctioned off in 1869 and subsequently demolished.

George Balmford, dyer and cleaner (famous for being the first business in York to install a telephone, linking Coney Street with his North Street factory), Leak & Thorpe and Thomas Horsley, gunsmith took its place. The colour painting, by S.C. Maggs, shows the George during York Races – similar scenes of consternation can sometimes be seen in Coney Street today when the races are in town.

Winn's George about 1920. The two pillars on the right are all that remain ... (Evelyn Collection, courtesy of Yorkshire Architectural and York Archaeological Society)

Famous guests included Vanbrugh, and Anne and Charlotte Brontë in May 1849, en route to Scarborough; they shopped and visited the Minster. Four days later, Anne died of consumption aged twenty-nine. It had a large galleried quadrangle, and a highly decorated frontage with elaborate plasterwork. Any remnants are now buried under 'Next'.

John Taylor, the Water Poet, stayed here in 1622 and waxed lyrical in his *A very merrie, wherry –ferry voyage or York for my money*. Elsewhere, he praised the landlord: 'to honest Mr Kayes in Cunneystreet. He entertan'd me well, for which I thank him, And gratefully amongst my friends I'll rank him.'

Gimcrack, Fulford Road – Before it was a pub (from 1936) it was a private residence. Gimcrack was a grey, by Cripple out of Miss Elliot winning twenty-seven out of thirty-five races, but never at York. The Ancient Fraternitie of Gimcracke was founded in 1770 in York in his honour, now the Gimcrack Club. The Gimcrack Stakes is run at the Knavesmire.

Glassmakers Arms, Fawcett Street.

Named after, and to serve, the local glassmaking industry. Previous names include the York Glass Works, the York Glass House, the (York) Glass Makers' Arms.

The first glassworks was opened in 1794 by Hampston and Prince near Fishergate making flint glass and medicinal phials. The York Flint Glass Company was set up in 1835 and by 1851 was a bigger employer than either confectioners Terry or Craven. In 1930 it was incorporated as National Glass Works (York) Ltd, which became Redfearn National Glass Company in 1967; it was demolished in 1988 and has been replaced by the Novotel.

Globe, Shambles – 1666. Later to become a private house.

Seen in 1989.

Glovers' Arms, Goodramgate – 1823. It may also have been the Queen Caroline. Later, it was the Grove, the Gardners' Arms and the Eagle.

Golden Barrel, Walmgate – 1649. Criminals on the way to the gallows at Green Dykes were given mint water here.

Gotty's, Love Lane – It was named after landlord Albert Gott; familiar name for the New Walk Tavern.

Grandstand, Knavesmire – Owned by the York Race Committee.

Great Northern, George Hudson Street – Built to coincide with North Midland Railway Company's new road linking Micklegate with the station (York's second) at Toft Green in 1843. It lasted into the 60s when the top storey was removed and it became the

Pageant, complete with disco lights and loud music. This led to a loss of licence and a change to the Merlin, bereft of said lights and music, allegedly. It changed back to the Great Northern in 1984.

Grapes, King Street (First Water Lane until 1852) – Formerly the Black Boy.

Greyhound, Spurriergate – 1772. No WC for customers.

Grid Iron, Lendal – 1824. The attribute of St Leonard at the nearby hospital. Also called the Coffee House.

Grob & Ducat, Rougier Street – Richard III in 1980.

Ham & Barrel, Walmgate.

Ham & Firkin, Walmgate – 1761. The name may be a reference to York's famous ham. York Ham is a dry-cured ham; according to legend, it obtained its unique flavour from the sawdust from the oak timbers used in the building of York Minster. However, York hams have never been smoked, although they are distinguished by the fact that the pigs' legs are long cut – they are rounded at the hip rather than squared off. *Law's Grocer's Manual* of 1949 tells us that 'In England the principal ham is long-cut, pale-dried dry-salt cured ham known as York Ham'.

Hand & Heart, St Sampson's Square.

Hand & Whip, Castlegate – 1770.

Harry's Café Bar, Micklegate – 1984.

Haymarket, Haymarket.

Hole in the Wall, High Petergate – Next to the Chapel of St Sepulchre where the Minster Library is now.

Hole in the Wall, Pump Yard – The easily missable Pump Yard is at the junction of King's Court and Newgate. John Wesley preached in a room here, which he referred to as the 'Oven' in 1753 (one of twenty-six visits to the city) 'through the multitude of people'; the home of a John Elwick, it became an official place of worship for Methodists in 1754. Two men, Samuel Stow (mariner) and Samuel Penrose (wheelwright) were 'held to bail for purposefully and contemptuously disturbing the congregation'. Before this, services were held in the Spartan Countess of Huntingdon's Chapel in 1751 and in 1752 in a building that

Half Moon Hotel, Blake Street – Around 1920. (Evelyn Collection, courtesy of Yorkshire Architectural and York Archaeological Society)

(Courtesy and © of York Press)

was to become the Hole in the Wall pub. The building was still there in 1957: a plaque tells us that the upper storey was a meeting place between 1753 and 1759 and that the room in which the Methodists met was wrecked by fire in 1880. John Wesley preached here twice—on 9 May 1753 and 5 June 1755—and Charles Wesley twice in October 1756. One of the country's only two surviving lantern tower windows is in Pump Court, tragically, almost hidden from public view. Betty Petre lived here; she kept her cattle in the court before slaughter in Shambles; Mr Huber collected sheep's guts and washed them in a drain before exporting them to Germany to make fiddle strings. Other residents included a chimney sweep and a prostitute, referred to locally as 'an old knock'. The Methodist room now serves as offices.

Imperial, Crichton Avenue – 1937.

Jacob's Well, Trinity Lane – 1822. The name aptly derives from Jacob's Well in biblical Samaria. According to the website in answer to the question, 'what is the significance of Jacob's Well?' (www.gotquestions.org/Jacobs-well.html):

> In chapter 4 of his Gospel, John recorded the story of Jesus talking with the Samaritan woman. Samaria was located in the northern half of the formerly united Israel, and Jesus was passing through it on His way from Judea to Galilee. Outside the town of Sychar, 'Jacob's well was there, and Jesus, tired as he was from the journey, sat down by the well' (John 4:6). He asked a woman to give Him something to drink from what she drew (John 4:7), and she wondered why a Jewish man would speak to a Samaritan woman—Jesus was breaking a cultural taboo because of both race and gender (John 4:9). Jesus then offered her 'living water' (John 4:10). This confused her, and she responded, 'Where can you get this living water? Are you greater than our father Jacob, who gave us the well and drank from it himself, as did also his sons and his flocks and herds?' (John 4:11–12).

Jacob's Well was a 15th century timber-framed house in Trinity Lane off Micklegate. Around 1600 the house was converted into a two-storey building. Originally a coach house, it became an inn from 1750 to 1903 called *The Jacob's Well*. The inn consisted of a bar and a smoke room, and a taproom used as dining-room-cum-kitchen. Accommodation for the resident licensee was upstairs. The licence was eventually surrendered and transferred to a new public house in Nunnery Lane. In the early

1800s the innkeeper added a third storey in brick, thus over-loading the timber frame below. The Church acquired the property in 1904; the entrance in Trinity Lane was improved by the addition of carved entrance porch brackets and canopy obtained from the Wheatsheaf Inn in Davygate, formerly the town house of the Bishop of Durham. York Butcher's Guild now use Jacob's Well as their Guild Hall.

John Bull, Layerthorpe – 1902.

Jolly Bacchus, High Ousegate – 1666. Bacchus, of course, was the Roman deity associated with wine and vine, and the celebrations that would often ensue from its consumption. The cult of Bacchus was originally exclusively female, and famous for its harmless ostentation; the frenzied shrieking of its adherents, the cacophonous banging of drums and the clashing of cymbals, and dressing up flamboyantly. The cult had a huge popular appeal amongst women even before men were admitted. The rite was a relatively relaxed and benign affair, with daytime celebrations three times a year, and the priestesses were dependable *matronae*. Things changed dramatically when a Campanian priestess called Paculla Annia began initiating men – the rites were moved to night-time performances, they began taking place a more-frequent five times a month, and membership was restricted to people aged twenty and under. Livy described its spread as an epidemic that excited sexual emotion in women. Plutarch tells us that frenzied women went straight for the ivy, chewing on it to bring on 'a wineless drunkenness and joyousness; [it] has an exciting and distracting breath of madness, deranges persons, and agitates them' – a veritable rave. Officially, the rite was seen as the manifestation of an unsettling conspiracy against Rome; one of the founding Etruscan initiates was suspected of occult activity, mysterious nocturnal sacrifices, and soothsaying. The 7,000 members were bound by an oath that committed them to fornication and crime. The heady mix of wine, darkness, women, and men was explosive, resulting in *orgia* on a grand scale – providing a springboard for perjury, forgery, poisoning and murder. Traditionalists saw the initiation of men as tantamount to removing them from their rightful place in the sanctity of the home, the family and the state.

Jacob's Well (Evelyn Collection, courtesy of Yorkshire Architectural and York Archaeological Society)

Jonah Landed, Coppergate – 1733. It marked the place where York carriers mustered. The name was inspired by 'And the Lord commanded the fish, and it vomited Jonah onto dry land' (Jonah 2:10).

Julius Caesar, Petergate – 1754.

Junction, Leeman Road – Railway associations.

Kavern Club, Micklegate – Or Cellar Club. York in the 60s had its own home-grown music scene with venues like the Kavern Club, the Mandrake in Stonegate, and Neil Guppy's Enterprise Club hosting live music by young city bands. Some of it started in the 50s, but much of it persisted throughout the 60s or originated in that decade. The Kavern Club started life as a coffee bar; it was in the basement of the Labour Party headquarters, appropriately decorated with graffiti. By 1964 there were 100 or so local groups performing in the city: allegedly, the crime rate fell because most young people were either performing in groups or watching them.

The Kavern Club in 1964 in Micklegate. (Photos courtesy and © of York Press)

When psychedelia became cool, York's main protagonists were Roll Movement, Angel Pavement, and the Smoke. Roll Movement supported names like Cream, The Who and Pink Floyd.

Keel, King's Staith – Once a beerhouse called the Old Ouse Bridge, the New Bridge and the Labour in Vain. There was a Keel in Marygate too from 1818.

King of Prussia, North Street – 1770.

King's Head, Foss Bridge in the early 1920s; closed in 1936 and the licence transferred to the Gimcrack Hotel. The building jutting out on the right down the road is the Queen's Head Hotel, which was closed in 1956.

Knife & Steel, Swinegate – 1795.

Leeds Arms, Peasholme Green – 1827. Previously the Clifford's Tower. It was closed in 1935; it was finally demolished in 1966.

Black Swan and Leeds Arms around 1905 on the right. The boy on
the left? A ghost from the Black Swan? (Evelyn Collection, courtesy of
Yorkshire Architectural and York Archaeological Society)

Leeman Hotel, Stamford Street – This pub was named after George Leeman
(1809–1882), lawyer and Liberal MP twice for the City of York. In 1849 he was
chairman of the York, Newcastle and Berwick Railway, succeeding the 'Railway
King' George Hudson after he helped uncover Hudson's illegal share dealing.
Leeman was deputy chairman of North Eastern Railways from 1855–1874 and
chairman from 1874—1880. He was Lord Mayor three times.

Lendal Bridge Hotel, Tanners Moat – Once
the Railway Tavern.

Leopard, Coney Street – 1778. Destroyed
in the 1942 Baedeker raid. The raids on
York, Norwich, Bath, Canterbury and
Exeter became known as Baedeker because
Goring's staff allegedly used the famous
travel guide to select their *Vergeltungsangriffe*
(retaliatory) targets – namely 3*** English
cities – in retaliation for the RAF destruction
of Lubeck and Rostock. Seventy German
bombers, largely unopposed, bombed
York for two hours: eighty-six people died
including fourteen children, and ninety-
eight were seriously injured (not including
undisclosed army and RAF fatalities). In
total, 9,500 houses (30 per cent of the city's
stock) were damaged or destroyed leaving
2,000 people homeless. The Guildhall and
St Martin le Grand Church were also badly damaged. The Bar Convent School
collapsed, killing five nuns including the headmistress, Mother Vincent. The

following day the *Daily Mail* reported: 'The gates of York still stand high, like the spirit of its people who, after nearly two hours of intense bombing and machine-gunning, were clearing up today.' There is a plaque on York Railway Station in honour of Station Foreman William Milner who died in the raid while entering a burning building to get medical supplies. His body was found still holding the box; he was posthumously awarded the King's Commendation for Gallantry.

The Lion & Lamb in 1965.

Lion & Lamb, Blossom Street (later the Nickel & Dime) – 1783.

Locomotive, Watson Street – 1851.

London Coffee House, Feasegate – 1825.

London Hotel, Davygate.

Londsbro Arms, 52 Low Petergate.

Lord John Cavendish, Fossgate – This pub was named after Lord John Cavendish PC (1732–1796), youngest son of William Cavendish, 3rd Duke of Devonshire; he was Chancellor of the Exchequer in 1782 and 1783.

Lord Nelson – There were Lord Nelsons in Goodramgate, High Jubbergate, Little Shambles, Navigation Road, Nether Poppleton, Patrick Pool, Swinegate and Walmgate.

Lottery, St Nicholas' Place, Hull Road – 1840.

Magpie, Penly's Grove Street. Also known as the Magpie & Stump – 1838.

Mariner, Far Water Lane – 1783.

Market Tavern, Coppergate – Once the Leopard. Ex-Sergeant Major Culham of the 9th Lancers won the licence only to be sacked by Tadcaster Tower Breweries when he pawned it and concern over his 'slack ways'. Now it is Russell's Restaurant.

(The Sign of The) Maypole, Clifton Green – Named after the maypole that stood there. Sadly, there is more to its reputation than the innocent pleasure of dancing round a decorated pole. In 1647 sisters Elizabeth and Helen Drysdale were executed at York for poisoning the beer of their lovers here with oxalic acid; the men died, the girls were hanged and the girls' bodies were later given up for anatomical dissection. In 1649 another

The Market Tavern. Note the dangerous proximity of the gun store. (Evelyn Collection, courtesy of Yorkshire Architectural and York Archaeological Society)

woman was hanged after being found guilty of burning down the pub.

Neptune, Micklegate.

Newcastle Arms, George Street – Once the Craven Ox Head and the Craven Ox.

North Eastern Refreshment Inn, Tanner Row – Once the Railway Coffee House and the Refreshment Inn. In 1879 it was the Railway Inn and then the Grapes.

Old Malt Shovel, Walmgate – 1828. Originally a Betts Brothers Brewery house. This was at No. 12; there was another Old Malt Shovel at No. 66, which became the Spread Eagle.

Old Rackitt, Petergate/Swinegate – 1694.

Old Turk's Head, King's Square.

Pack Horse, Shambles – Pack Horses also in Micklegate (2), Skeldergate, Fossgate, Pavement, Skeldergate, Askham Bryan.

Pageant, George Hudson Street – Previously, it was the Great Northern Hotel.

Painted Wagon, Piccadilly. This was a pub built under the converted ABC cinema in 1972.

Parrot, Walmgate and **Little Shambles.**

Paviers, St Dennis Parish.

Pewterer's Arms, Low Ousegate – 1783.

Pig & Whistle, Newgate – 1838.

Pink Pony Fun Pub, Gillygate.

Ploughboy's Rest, Swinegate – 1849.

Plumber's Arms, Skeldergate – This was a fine 16th century building (1575) with a grand fireplace, 17th century panelling and an 18th century staircase. Alas, in 1965 it was all taken down but thankfully the best bits were incorporated into the new Cock & Bottle, which was later the Villiers before reverting to the Cock & Bottle.

One of the Packhorse pubs in Micklegate – this one is Riley's in about 1915. (Evelyn Collection, courtesy of Yorkshire Architectural and York Archaeological Society)

Painted Wagon, Piccadilly. (Courtesy and © of York Press)

The Pink Pony Club, Gillygate

Printing Press, Swinegate – Once the Stanhope Press. It reflects the printing and publishing in the area. Printing came to England in 1477 with William Caxton and is first recorded in York in 1497 when Fridericus Freez, an immigrant 'docheman' is noted as 'Book Bynder' and 'Stationer' and later as a 'Buke Printer'. Hugo Goez set up in 1509 and Thomas Gent (d. 1778) published scores of chap books from Coffee Yard. Grace White was the first woman to publish a newspaper here in 1718, *The York Mercury,* in Coffee Yard with Thomas Hammond, Quaker bookseller; the paper passed to Thomas Gent in 1724. Another Quaker, William Alexander, opened a bookselling business in Castlegate in 1811 expanding into printing in 1814. This was eventually taken over by William Sessions in 1865, surviving until 2009. Ben Johnson and Co. Ltd was established as a lithographic printer by Johnson and John Lancaster, specialising in railway timetables and other jobs associated with the railways. John Glaisby's bookshop and library was in Coney Street; in 1848 it had been the premises of William Hargrove's *York Herald*, next to the George Hotel and known then as Kidd's Coffee House. Hargrove bought it from Caesar Ward, owner of the 1750 established Whig *York Courant,* in 1815; the *Courant* had been moved there from the Bagnio by Ann Ward, Caesar's widow. The magnificent statues and the bust and books have sadly gone, although the publishing heritage of the building was extended when it became the offices of the then *York Evening Press* (1882) and the *Yorkshire Gazette and Herald* (which changed from a weekly in 1874 and absorbed the *Courant* in 1848). Ward was also the publisher of the first edition of Laurence Sterne's *The Life and Opinions of Tristram Shandy.* F.R. Delittle, at the Eboracum Letter Factory, in Railway Street was founded in 1888.

Queen's Head Hotel, Fossgate – 1838. Once the Wellington Coffee House.

Queen's Head Hotel, Fossgate in the left foreground. (Evelyn Collection, courtesy of Yorkshire Architectural and York Archaeological Society)

An intact medieval roof was one of the many casualties when this building, housing the Queen's Head Hotel, Fossgate was destroyed by planners.

Railway King, George Hudson Street – Formerly the Adelphi.

Rat Pit, Carmelite Street – A nickname for the Garden Gate.

Recruiting Serjeant, Trinity Lane – 1783.

Reindeer, Penley's Grove Street – A beerhouse previously known as the Highland (Red) Deer.

Richard III – Corner of Rougier Street and Tanner Row – formerly the Grob and Ducat and then the Ebor Café from 1893 to 1974

Robin Hood/Little John/ Blue Boar, Castlegate – Now the Blue Boar.

Sailor with a Wooden Leg, Low Ousegate – After an early 19th century sketch used for a pub sign, possibly at the Mariner on King's Staith.

Sanctuary, 68 Gillygate.

Sawdust 'Ole, King's Square – A familiar name for the Grapes.

Sawdust Parlour, Swinegate – Originally a stable and then a meeting place for carvers and artists.

Scawin's Railway Hotel, Tanner Row – During the days of the stage coach, travellers stayed at coaching inns when they broke or ended their journeys. The emerging railway companies soon realised that this was not the answer to rail travellers' accommodation needs – something very close to the station was required. And so the station hotel was born. Indeed, the early railway hotels were actually the first travel packages: rail and hotel, city breaks.

The Old Station in Tanner Row was complemented by a hotel that was built at the head of the rails; it opened in February 1853 to a design by Andrews. Fittingly, it was originally called The Station Hotel and had fifteen reception rooms and fifty-five bedrooms. It became known as Scawin's Railway Hotel after Sarah Scawin bought it in 1854 with it bearing her name long after she sold it in 1869; it was demolished in 1900 after the new hotel at the new railway station became well established. Scawin's could boast as one of its guests Queen Victoria who stayed there in September 1854.

Ship, 5 King's Staith – 1787. Over the years there have been fourteen pubs in York named Ship, and four Slips. Not bad for a land-locked city; it reflects the importance of the rivers here and, in the case of Strensall, the navigation.

Soldier's Rest Inn, Fulford Road – 1867.

Sportsman, Hungate – Once the Dog & Gun. There were more Sportsmans in Caroline Street and Hungate.

Spotted Dog, Walmgate – 1822.

The middle building is Petty's
Star & Garter, in 1896.

Star & Garter, Nessgate – The middle building is Petty's Star & Garter, in 1896.

Steam Hammer, Skeldergate.

Talbot, Church Street – There were more Talbots in Spurriergate, Low Petergate and Micklegate.

Tang Hall Hotel, Fourth Avenue – 1930.

Tavern in the Town, Ouse Bridge – 1958. It was a former brewery, then a pub exhibiting features of many different periods, replete with paraphernalia.

Tin Chicken Club, New Earswick – In late 1966 the visionary management of the Tin Chicken Club at New Earswick's Folk Hall booked a little-known band called The Paramounts to play at one of their regular Saturday night concerts some months down the line. Just before the gig in 1967, The Paramounts released a single called *A Whiter Shade of Pale* and changed their name to the faux Latin Procol Harum. The Move, Pink Floyd and Ike and Tina Turner are said to have played there as well.

Three Legs of Man, Monkgate – The Three Legs of Man were adopted in the 13th century as the royal coat of arms for three kings of the Isle of Man whose realm at the time also included the Hebrides in the Western Isles of Scotland. The emblem was kept when control of the Island passed permanently to the English Crown. The history of the Three Legs goes as far back as pagan times and was originally a symbol of the sun and of power and life.

Tower of London, Haymarket – Once the Shoulder of Mutton.

Trafalgar Bay, Nunnery Lane – 1834. It closed in 2017. It commemorated the Battle of Trafalgar on 21 October 1805 – the pivotal naval engagement fought by the British against the fleets of the French and Spanish Navies, during the War of the Third Coalition (August–December 1805) of the Napoleonic Wars (1796–1815).

Twenty-seven British ships of the line led by Admiral Lord Nelson on HMS *Victory* defeated thirty-three French and Spanish ships of the line under the French Admiral Villeneuve off the southwest coast of Spain, just west of Cape Trafalgar. The Franco–Spanish fleet lost twenty-two ships, without a single British loss. It was the most decisive naval battle of the war. During the battle, Nelson was shot by a French musketeer; he died soon after.

Trumpet, Town End Street.

Turf Tavern, Thanet Road – Three more in Tadcaster Road, Railway View and Market Street with Turf Coffee Houses in Davygate and Jubbergate.

Turk's Head, St Andrewgate – Formerly the Saracen's Head. Four more Turk's Heads crop up in College Street, King's Square, Low Ousegate and Petergate. There were Turk's Head coffee shops in Coney Street, King's Square and Low Ousegate.

By 1675, there were apparently more than 3,000 coffee houses in England alone. Some had bed and breakfast for overnight guests. Many, as in York, seemed to follow the same Turkish coffee house-type business model if their exotic names are anything to go by. We can only speculate on how many were actually run by Muslims or immigrants from the Levant. There were up to fifty-seven different 'Turk's Head' coffee houses; 'The Jerusalem Coffee-house'; various types of the 'Blackamoor' or 'Ye Blackmore's Head'; 'The Oriental Cigar Divan'; 'The Saracen's Head' (of Dickens fame); 'The Africa and Senegal Coffee-house'; 'The Sultaness'; 'The Sultan's Head'; 'Solyman's Coffee House'; and 'Morat Ye Great'.

Two Angels, Marygate – 1770.

Unicorn – Four York public houses have had this name, the Unicorn in Lord Mayor's Walk is first recorded in 1852; it had four bedrooms, a taproom and smoke room, and the family there shared their toilet facilities with the customers. York Interment Institution held a meeting here in 1852. It closed in 1956. The other Unicorns were in Monkgate (the 1791– 1846 Malton coaching inn), Petergate (flourishing around the 1780s) and Tanner Row (from 1804–1985).

The Unicorn in Lord Mayor's Walk. (Evelyn Collection, courtesy of Yorkshire Architectural and York Archaeological Society)

Upholsterer's Arms – Or the Upholder's Arms, Trinity Lane.

Whale Fishery, Carmelite Street.

White Horse, Pavement. Isabella Campbell and Caroline Nicholson were two nineteen-year-old women of easy virtue on their way back from the York Horse Fair in 1853 when they came upon John Hall staggering out of the White Horse in Pavement flush with drink and with the proceeds from selling his horse at the fair. The women pounced and led him down to King's Staith and the icy cold River Ouse en route to their lodgings. Inevitably, Hall ended up in the river and the women repaired to McGregor's Dram Shop on Low Ousegate; Hall's body was found downstream near the public washing area known as Pudding Holes; the women were arrested in Nessgate. A purse was found on Isabella Campbell. At the Guildhall magistrates the women were remanded in the House of Correction at Toft Green and later convicted of the wilful murder of John Hall.

White Rose, Cornlands Road, Acomb.

White Rose Inn, Jubbergate. Originally Joubrettagate – the Street of the Bretons in the Jewish Quarter – and Jubretgate. Over the years occupants have included Webster's kitchen and bath-ware shop, which became Pawson's, specialists in rubber-ware; The White Rose Inn became Forrington's furnishers around 1920. At one stage in its life it was home to six families. Jubbergate originally extended to cover what is today Market Street as far as Coney Street. York's first police station was here until 1880 when it moved to Clifford Street.

White Swan, Pavement.

The old Lowis's White Swan Hotel on Pavement, just before it was demolished so that Piccadilly could be extended to link up with Pavement and Parliament Street in 1912. *The York Press* (27 November 2017) tells us that the

> extension had first been proposed in May 1907. It was suggested that the new street would give new frontages and the city sheriff, Councillor Meyer, believed that the street could be laid out in such a way that the new frontage would pay for the improvements. Deputy Mayor Alderman Agar and Councillor Walker are recorded as being opposed to the scheme as they feared it would ruin Fossgate.

Wild Man, Petergate, 1727. And another in Water Lane, and another on the A64 approaching Tadcaster. Notorious as a haunt of thieves and highwaymen, it was possibly originally called The Bush or something similar if the depositions of York Castle in 1675 are to be believed: Abraham Ibbotson of Leeds was charged with stealing horses, the felonious act being plotted at an ale house in Street Houses 'in the way betwixt Tadcaster and York where there was a bush as a signe'. The bush was associated with the Roman god Bacchus who was often depicted as a wild man on account of his characteristic state of frenzy and intoxication; the two symbols have become virtually synonymous. Legend has it that the almost life-size sign was covered up when Queen Victoria passed by *en route* to York with white calico 'so that the Queen might not be shocked at the sight of so hairy (and naked) a man'. Nowadays, the Aaghra provides refreshment of a less erotic, more exotic nature.

William Bass, Market Street, (Evelyn Collection, courtesy of Yorkshire Architectural and York Archaeological Society)

William Bass, Market Street – The Tiger until 1988; licensed in 1851 next door to the Hansom Cab (Burns Hotel). The name, of course, honours the founder of the Bass Brewery in 1750.

Windmill, Wigginton – First recorded in 1857. It was popularly known as the Mill. Mill Lane here is named after the mill that stood on Sutton Road opposite the Shipton Road junction, now the site of Windmill House and the Windmill Trading Estate. It features on the 1769 enclosure map. The Windmill public house was next door, demolished in 1930. In 1906 revenues from the land in Wigginton amounted to £11.00; 6s.8d of which was paid for tithe, 30s to 10 deserving poor and the rest for the services of the parish bull who performed in the Bull Field, now

The Windmill, Wigginton. Originally published in Hugh Murray's *A Directory of York Pubs.*

Mill Lane playing field. In 1791 the fee per cow was 1s; the last bull came (literally) and went in 1952.

Windmill Inn, St George's Field on the Foss – Records of its existence date from 1782.

Windmill Inn. (Evelyn Collection, courtesy of Yorkshire Architectural and York Archaeological Society)

Compulsory archery training for all males took place at the butts here. It was a public place for hanging out washing to dry. The second photo is from 1855. Around 1275 the grand military order of the powerful Knights Templar owned a mill here (Castle Mills) and chapel; abuse of power and prodigious wealth, however, in the 14th century, led to the seizure of their land and property by the Crown. The lower stonework on the old Windmill pub is, in fact, the original stonework from the chapel. It was all demolished in 1856 to create the Foss Basin and improve river access to the glassworks on the opposite bank. The works themselves were later demolished to be replaced by the Novotel.

St George's Fields was the location of the York ducking stool – for scoundrels and women who sold short measures or bad beer and 'scolds and flyters'. The gallows nearby attracted large crowds, some coming by special train excursions as late as 1862. There were heated baths here from 1879 to 1972: they comprised separate men's and women's baths and a bath for York residents without a bath at home who could come and bathe there.

Yearsley Grove, Huntington Road – First a house, then a hotel and, after World War II, a pub.

York Golf Club House, Knavesmire – The original club house was built in 1907; York Golf Club was founded in 1890 at the Knavesmire. The fact that it was on public land caused problems: cows, horses and other livestock grazed on land also frequented by nursemaids with their perambulators. One of the early club rules was indicative of the hazards: 'Members are to refrain from striking while people or cattle are in the way.' An early guide described it as 'apt to be sticky'.

To avoid accidents to man and beast the Club moved to what was army land in Strensall in 1904. The Army has always been important to the Club as illustrated by the fact that the Presidency is always held by the senior officer of the York garrison. A clear-out in the Club in 1960 revealed a large number of old golf bags and clubs – some of which had not been collected by soldiers who failed to return from the Great War.

Yorkshire Hussar, North Street – A pub since 1808 that was rebuilt in 1896. In 1808 it was a butcher's shop and was the Yorkshire Tavern after 1843.

CLOSING TIME

In April 2015 CAMRA announced the results of its survey to find the country's best 200 community pubs. CAMRA have been judging pubs for decor, value for money, customer service and, of course, the quality of their beer.

For Yorkshire the list includes: Barnsley: Old No 7; Bradford: Jacobs Beer House; Doncaster: Corner Pin; Halifax: Three Pigeons; Harrogate: Harrogate Tap; Mirfield: Flower Pot; Huddersfield: Grove Inn; Beverley: Chequers Micropub; Keighley: Brown Cow; Leeds: Kirkstall Bridge Inn; Hawes: White Hart Country Inn; Rotherham: Beehive; Pickering: Sun Inn; Sheffield: Kelham Island Tavern; Castleford: Junction; York: Maltings.

For what it's worth, here is my list of the top eleven pubs in York city centre, in no particular order:

The Maltings	The Golden Fleece	The York Tap
The Blue Bell	Ye Olde Starre Inn	The Golden Ball
The Ackhorne	The Black Swan	The House of the
The Golden Slipper	The Red Lion	Trembling Madness

The Black Swan

The Red Lion (Evelyn Collection, courtesy of Yorkshire Architectural and York Archaeological Society)

The Landlord, by FW Elwell (1870–1958), in Ferens Art Gallery, Hull.

York City Pub Crawl produced by York Brewery (© Bernie Carroll Publications 2014)

APPENDIX:
STRANGE AND ECCENTRIC
YORKSHIRE PUB NAMES

Some of Yorkshire's pub names are odd, arcane and obscure. Here are a few of the puzzling ones, in no particular order, although we might as well begin with The Puzzle Hall at Sowerby Bridge, which denotes the puzzles inside available to drinkers, which puzzled all. The Folly outside Halifax remembers the 270 feet high folly built by John E. Wainhouse to annoy his neighbour. The Salmon Leap (formerly The Station Hotel) at Sleights denotes the salmon leap on the River Esk there, while The Three Legs of Man in Leeds describes the Isle of Man coat of arms. Hull's Goat and Compasses is a corruption of the Puritan motto 'God encompasses us' while the city's Ravenser remembers the village on the Humber engulfed by the sea in 1346. Bell ringing is commemorated in The Ring of Bells in Barnsley. The nickname (Peter) of the landlady of The Just Peter Inn (once The Railway Inn) provides the name for this curious pub in Holme on Spalding Moor. Between York and Malton is The Spitalbeck Inn, but there is no beck to be seen: the original inn was next to the Spital Beck a mile down the road at Barton Hill. In earlier times coaches would stop at the inn to collect two fresh horses to help the existing team haul its load to the top of the much steeper hill. Part of the building that became the inn was used as a hospital for Cromwellian soldiers during the siege at Scarborough Castle in the Civil War. Despite the image painted on its sign The Bruce Arms at West Tanfield has nothing to do with Robert the Bruce; it was originally named after the Bruce family, famous northern landowners. The Triangle Inn in Sowerby Bridge is vaguely mathematical, named as it is after the triangular piece of land on which the nearby village of Triangle is situated. In Triangle itself is The White Bear: the Triangle Cricket Club was founded at the pub as was the Triangle Reading Society; the pub was used as a Coroner's Court. Other White Bears prowl around Barnsley, Masham, Sowerby Bridge, Skircoat Green and, confusingly, Cow Green in Halifax. One bear that did no prowling was The Old White Beare at Norwood Green near Halifax from 1533: this pub was named after a ship that fought the Spanish Armada. There was a Leopard in York slain by the Luftwaffe in the 1942 Baedeker raid; and one in Calverley (later The Thornhill Arms) dating back to 1673 and named after the three leopards on the coat of arms of the Weavers' Company. North of York, Haxby and the contiguous village of Wigginton are a veritable safari park with their Tiger, Red Lion and Black Horse. Another Tiger was in Hedon; there is a Blue Lion at East Witton. The Wolf in Luddenden, built in 1653, was said to be a rendezvous for army recruiting officers in the early 18th century; in 1745,

Janet, a Scottish maid at the inn gave sanctuary to a soldier from Bonnie Prince Charlie's army who was being pursued by the English army. In 1877, the property was acquired by the Luddenden Co-operative Society; the Luddenden Working Men's Club & Institute was also here from 1880 until 1946. Foxes abound, with or without the hounds; one Fox is in Holgate in York, another was in Low Petergate dating from the 15th century but demolished in 1958; its other names were The Lord Byron and The Beech Tree.

Here are some quintessentially Yorkshire-named Yorkshire pubs. The Wapping Spring brewery and the spring that watered it in Outlane just outside Huddersfield gave its name to The Wappy Spring Inn. The brewery closed in 1957. The Who Could A' Thowt It in Brighouse was the Masons' Arms until 1870. The Who Could A' Thowt It in Southowram was formerly Clough Head Cottage at Clough Head, Sunny Bank Lane and also known pithily as Who Would a Thowt It, Ba Gum Who'd A' Thowt It, and Ba Gum Who Wad A' Thowt It in the 1860s. There was a passage between the cellars of the pub and the cottage next door, which provided a quick escape for illegal drinkers. The pub closed in 1933; when it was demolished the stone and roof slates went into the rebuilding of Coventry after World War II. The Queen O'Towd Thatch at South Milford dates from 1720 and means nothing more than the queen with an old thatched roof – a feature that endured until the early 1900s. The Ram's Head at Denshaw was popularly known as T'Owd Tupps. The Needless got its name from the magistrate (depicted on the sign) who declared that another pub on the Morley–Batley road was 'needless' as there were already two. Needless prevailed, however, and became one of the many pubs in which Dick Turpin downed his last pint before incarceration. It was also called The Cardigan Arms. The Q in the Corner in Sheffield was famous for its blind fiddlers while The Warm Hearthstone nearby was well known for encouraging drinkers to dip their own bread into dripping from the pub's roasts. In Barnsley, The Gyngleboy is named after the slang term for a coin and later for someone who jingles coins in their pocket. The Tom Treddlehoyle at Pogmoor was local author Charles Roger's pen name. The uniquely titled 18th century Lettered Board is in Pickering on Smiddy Hill.

The Samuel Plimsoll in Sheffield commemorates the man who saved many a seafarer's life when he did away with the 'coffin ships' and introduced his famous load line. Another life-saver is remembered by The Davy Lamp at Thrybergh near Rotherham. A male version of Knaresborough's Mother Shipton has been awarded eternal life in the sign of The Hermit Inn at Burley in Wharfedale (formerly The Woolpack): the hermit in question is the prophesying Job Senior – the bastard son of a wealthy Ilkey landowner born in 1780. Senior also had the special skill of being able to sing tenor, treble, alto and bass all in the same hymn. When his wife died, he was blamed and her relatives destroyed his house and stole all his money leaving him no choice but to become a hermit. The Henry Jenkins Inn at Kirby Malzeard remembers the man of that name who died in 1670 aged 169.

The Floating Light stood on the scenic A62 over Standedge; it opened in 1940 and closed around 2000. The name derives from lights used by workers digging the canal tunnel – the longest in Britain – that runs beneath. The Nont Sarah's pub at Scammonden above Huddersfield is named after Aunt Sarah, the licensee some 150 years ago. At Ogden The Causeway Foot used to be known as The Buck Inn, The Goose Inn and The Peat Pitts in 1789 after the nearby peat pitts. The Naked Man Inn in Settle dates from 1663; it is happily matched with The Naked Woman one mile up the road in Langliffe dating from 1660. Less happily both are long closed. The now shut Whale Fishery in York took its name from the licensee Christopher Bean who was a harpooner on Hull boats in the Arctic and created a vivid sign representing a miniature carved whaling boat. The Leeds coaching inn The Bull and Mouth was a corruption of Boulogne Mouth popularised by Henry VIII when he captured Boulogne Harbour. The Feoffees (try saying it after a few pints) in Sheffield was built on the site of a 1726 poor school – feoffees being the term for the charitable trustees. The Old Silent at Stanbury near Haworth gets its name from the fact that Bonnie Prince Charlie hid there and the locals maintained silence for a couple of weeks so that he could make good his escape.

In 1881 West Bottom Tavern in Halifax's Hob Lane was a row of three cottages for workers in the local quarries, the middle one of which was a beerhouse. The name was changed to The Hobbit after restoration in 1975. Also around Halifax T' Wheel Hoile was also known as Old Coley Mill Inn. It opened in 1830 and closed in the 1920s. The pub stood near Coley corn mill, which fell into disuse, leaving only the wheel hole once the dangerous mill wheel had been removed. The Whiskam Dandy was named after the hamlet of Whiskam Dandy. A less obvious railway hotel not called The Railway or The Station is the L. & Y.R. Hotel in Knottingley signifying the Lancashire and Yorkshire Railway. The Running Man in Halifax is a vivid reminder of the odious Halifax gibbet; freedom, and life, could we won by running a certain distance from the town. Failure, though, meant the gibbet after all and gave rise to the desperate refrain 'From Hull, Hell and Halifax, Good Lord Deliver Us'. There were four pubs called The New Delight around Halifax: one survives at Wanstalls; the name is taken from Milton's *Paradise Lost*: 'Heav'n's last best gift, my ever new delight' – Eve addressing Adam at Book V, 19. Once, it was called The Travellers' Rest. The Church Steps in Dewsbury is the only pub in Britain built on consecrated ground while The Postcard in Holmfirth is named after the comic post card firm, Balmforth, based there. The Flouch Inn from 1827 near Penistone is very odd: it was originally The New Inn but when the name was changed to The Plough, parts of the lettering, namely part of the p and part of the g, fell off ...

Pubs named after local industry and the occupations they spawned are, of course, extremely common, and we have already seen a number of Yorkshire examples. Here is a small selection of the less usual, some are gone, some are still with us: Brassmoulders Arms (Leeds); Boatman's Rest (Barnsley); Brickmakers Arms (Hull); Butchers Arms (Batley); Carriers Arms (Morley); Clothiers Arms (Leeds); The Cobblers (Pontefract); Colliers Arms (Elland); Coopers Arms, Jolly Sailors, Miners and Millers Arms, Hammer and Stithy – a name for an anvil (Ossett); Engineers Arms (Hull); Electricians Hotel (Huddersfield); Fellmongers Arms (Leeds); Foresters Arms and Graziers Arms (Wakefeld); Horsebreakers Arms (Hutton Sessay); Jet Miners Arms (Great Broughton); Joiners Arms (Hampsthwaite); Nailmakers Arms

(Sheffield); Ostlers Arms, Plasterers Arms and Skinners Arms (Leeds); Spinners Arms (Colne Bridge); Yarnspinners Arms (Bradford); Fishermans Hut (Leeds); Shepherd's Boy (Dewsbury); The Shears Inn (Hightown, Huddersfield).

The Plummet Line in Halifax opened in 1898 and still retains its fine tiled nameplate. It is, of course, named after the builders' weighted line. Halifax can also boast The Pot O' Four – the pot used by wool combers to heat their combs. The Whisket in Todmorden was originally a beerhouse built by William Fielden – a basket-maker; a whisket is a name for a basket. The Collier at Elland recalls the boats that shipped the coal and not the men who dug it; the nearby Barge and Barrel evokes similar memories. The Slubbers Arms in Huddersfield gets its name from slubber, a person or machine that slubs, i.e. works carelessly – here, a reference to textile workers. The Veterinary Arms at Hunmanby is so named after the vet who supplemented his fees with the selling of ale.

There is nothing unusual about the name of The Globe at Raistrick; however, in 1910 the landlord hanged himself during the lunchtime session; his wife carried on serving until the session was over before she called the police.

Less inviting pubs are: The World's End in Knaresborough – owned by Charles Blenkhorn, who also ran the nearby pleasure boats, hotel and café. He was also town postmaster; his sister was postmistress. At one time the pub sign is said to have depicted an earthquake with a bus falling into the River Nidd and the pub collapsing. The Cemetery Arms in Leeds and The Black Swan at Leyburn which has a man-trap on the wall are just as cheery. At South Kirby The Travellers doubled up as the village mortuary.

The Croppers Arms, Huddersfield

FURTHER READING

Aldabella, P. *Hull & East Yorkshire Breweries*, East Yorkshire Local History Society, Hull, 1997.

Baggs, A.P., G.H.R. Kent and J.D. Purdy, *A History of the County of York East Riding: Volume 3, Ouse and Derwent Wapentake, and Part of Harthill Wapentake*, ed. K.J. Allison, London, 1976. British History Online www.british-history.ac.uk/vch/yorks/east/vol3 [accessed 11 February 2018].

Brandon, D. *Discovering Pub Names and Signs*, Oxford, 2010.

Brandwood, G. *Licensed to Sell – The History and Heritage of the Public House*, 2nd edition, English Heritage, 2011.

Bruning, T. *Historic Pubs of England*, London, 2000.

CAMRA. *Real Ale in York: A Comprehensive Guide to Real Ale in the City of York*, 2nd edition. St Albans, 2010.

Chrystal, P. *Coffee: A Drink for the Devil*, Stroud, 2016.

Chrystal, P. *Harrogate Pubs including Knaresborough*, Stroud, 2016.

Chrystal, P. *Historic England: Hull*, Stroud, 2017.

Chrystal, P. *Hull in 50 Buildings*, Stroud, 2017.

Chrystal, P. *Hull Pubs*, Stroud, 2017.

Chrystal, P. *Old Yorkshire Country Life*, Catrine, 2017.

Chrystal, P. *The Place Names of Yorkshire, including Pub Names*, Catrine, 2017.

Chrystal, P. *The Rowntree Family of York*, Pickering, 2015.

Chrystal, P. *Yorkshire Murders, Murders, Manslaughter, Madness & Executions*, Catrine, 2018.

Clark, P. *The English Alehouse: A Social History 1200–1830*, London, 1983.

Cooper, T.P. *The Old Inns and Inn Signs of York*, York, 1897.

Coxon, P. *York's Historic Inns*, York, 1998.

Davis, B. *The Traditional English Pub: A Way of Drinking*, London, 1981.

Gamston, D. (ed.) *Yorkshire's Real Heritage Pubs: Pub Interiors of Special Historic Interest in Yorkshire and Humber, CAMRA*, St Albans, 2014.

Gamston, D. (ed.) *Historic Pubs in and Around York, CAMRA*, St Albans, 2004.

Girouard, M. *Victorian Pubs*, Yale, 1984.

Gorham, M. *Back to the Local*, London, 2007.

Gorham, M. *Inside the Pub*, London, 1950.

Haydon, P., *The English Pub: A History*, London, 1994.

Johnson, A. *The Inns and Alehouses of York*, Beverley, 1994.

Lister, P. *Ghosts and Gravestones of York*, Stroud, 2007.

Monckton, H.A. *A History of the English Public House*, London, 1969.

Monson-Fitzjohn, G.J. *Quaint Signs of Olde Inns*, London, 1926.

Murray. H.A. *Dictionary of York Pubs 1455–2003*, York, 2003.

Oliver, B. *The Renaissance of the English Public House*, London 1947.

Pepper, B. *A Haunt of Rare Souls*, Otley, 1990.

Pevsner, N. T*he Buildings of England: Yorkshire – York and the East Riding*, London, 1995.

Pickwell, W. *The Temperance Movement in the City of York, Its Origins, Basis and Progress*, York, 1886.

Race, M. *Public Houses, Private Lives: An Oral History of Life in York Pubs on the Mid-20th Century*, York, 1999.

Rowntree, B.S. *Poverty: A Study of Town Life*, London 1901.

Rowntree, Joseph, *The Temperance Problem and Social Reform, 1899; facs.* York, 2010.

Rowntree, Joseph, *Public Control of the Liquor Trade*, York,1903

Rowntree, Joseph, *The Taxation of the Liquor Trade*, York, 1906.

White, E. (ed.) *Feeding a City: York*, Tonbridge, 2000.

Websites

http://York.camra.org.uk

http://York.camra.org.uk/wp-content/uploads/2017/08/York-Pub-Map-July-2017.pdf

http://York.camra.org.uk/about-ouse-boozer/

https://pubheritage.camra.org.uk/home/home.asp?utm_medium=301&utm_source=heritagepubs.org.uk/home/home.asp

https://www.Yorkmix.com/food-drink/York-pubs-and-beer/guide-to-the-perfect-pint-14-of-Yorks-best-cask-ale-pubs/

www.theguardian.com/travel/2013/dec/12/York-top-ten-craft-beer-pubs

www.York-pm.co.uk/real-ale-pubs-York/

https://twitter.com/beerfestYork?lang=en

http://withinthewalls.tumblr.com/pubcrawls

www.issuu.com/York_archaeological_trust/docs/nat3-web/15